INSTAGRAM

The Best Business Strategy in Social Media

(Business Ideas for Newbie Online Marketers Instagram)

Ricardo Chandler

Published by Andrew Zen

Ricardo Chandler

All Rights Reserved

Instagram: The Best Business Strategy in Social Media
(Business Ideas for Newbie Online Marketers Instagram)

ISBN 978-1-989965-81-8

Legal & Disclaimer

The information contained in this book is not designed to replace or take the place of any form of medicine or professional medical advice. The information in this book has been provided for educational and entertainment purposes only.

The information contained in this book has been compiled from sources deemed reliable, and it is accurate to the best of the Author's knowledge; however, the Author cannot guarantee its accuracy and validity and cannot be held liable for any errors or omissions. Changes are periodically made to this book. You must consult your doctor or get professional medical advice before using any of the suggested remedies, techniques, or information in this book.

Upon using the information contained in this book, you agree to hold harmless the Author from and against any damages, costs, and expenses, including any legal fees potentially resulting from the application of any of the information provided by this guide. This disclaimer applies to any damages or injury caused by the use and application, whether directly or indirectly, of any advice or information presented, whether for breach of contract, tort, negligence, personal injury, criminal intent, or under any other cause of action.

You agree to accept all risks of using the information presented inside this book. You need to consult a professional medical practitioner in order to ensure you are both able and healthy enough to participate in this program.

Table of Contents

Introduction

The following chapters will discuss some of the many great steps that you can take to start your own business account on Instagram, and how to use this account to grow your business. Marketing on Instagram is great for businesses because it relies on pictures and videos, something that many customers enjoy looking at when it is time to make a decision on one of their purchases. You can fill this need with your potential customers by setting up a professional looking account with some great media that showcases your work.

This guidebook is going to help you get the most out of your Instagram account. We will talk about some of the benefits of using Instagram over some of the other social media accounts for growing your business, as well as how you can set up your own account. We also work on how to increase your presence on social media, how to get more followers on Instagram without having to pay an expensive professional, and some great tips to help you pick out the perfect pictures to entice more customers.

Instagram is the perfect social media site to help businesses to grow. And with some of the great tips that are inside this guidebook, you will be able to get your Instagram account off the ground while growing your business in no time.

There are plenty of books on this subject on the market, thanks again for choosing this one! Every effort was made to ensure it is full of as much useful information as possible. Please enjoy!

Chapter 1: Is Instagram Right For You?

We have already established the fact that Instagram is a very popular platform, and you might be missing a lot of opportunities if you are not in it yet. But like any other business decision, you should consider everything before you jump in.

Is Instagram the right channel for your online marketing? If so, what are the best strategies to market your brand on Instagram?

Sure. There are around 106 million Americans using the platform, which is a massive potential audience for you to grow, but there are pointers to consider to figure out if this channel is really suitable for your business.

What are the Age Demographics of Your Target Audience?

The main factor to consider is the fact that majority of Instagrammers are between 18 and 35 years old. Is this the ideal age range for your target audience? It makes sense for a fashion brand or a food chain to invest its resources to market on Instagram, but what if you're catering to the needs of retirees? Or what if your business mainly serves other businesses in your industry (B2B) such as IT solutions, accounting, or tax compliance?

If your target audience is not really within the age demographics of Instagrammers, this channel may not be on top of your priority platforms. This is a reality that you must carefully consider before you even sign up for an Instagram business account.

But if you have a retail brand that directly sells products to customers (B2C) or if your services primarily appeal to the younger audience, then it makes sense to build a massive presence on Instagram.

Can B2B Companies Use Instagram?

Yes, businesses that are offering products and services to other businesses can still use Instagram. The same goes for businesses that are not mainly catering to the needs of younger demographics. The key is to develop a content strategy that will effectively showcase your business or brand.

Remember, boosting sales is not the only benefit that Instagram can provide for your business. With the right strategy, you can use Instagram to share your company culture, allow exclusive access to behind-the-scene events, create an engaging platform for your employees, and many more.

Is Your Target Audience Mobile?

You also need to understand that Instagram is a mobile app. Hence, your audience can only see and engage with your brand if they are on mobile. Usually, those on Instagram are on the go, and they tend to be younger than facebook users who often check their accounts using desktop computers.

Does Your Audience Want Your Brand on Instagram?

If your target audience is on Instagram, the next factor to consider is the possibility that they want to see your brand on the platform. Based on a research conducted by GrowEpic, the top brands on Instagram are related to retail, food, beauty, and health.

However, your success on this platform is not strictly limited to your brand. Engaging content is still key. For example, NASA is far away from these industries, but they have around 14.1 million followers and one post can garner an average of 400,000 likes. You just need to really know your audience and share photos and videos that they want to see in their Instagram news feeds.

Do You Have the Skills and Resources to Effectively Use Instagram as a Marketing Platform?

Instagram is a powerful tool that will allow you to engage with your customers if you do it right. But before you can reap the rewards of customer engagement, you need to work hard on it. Again, engaging content is key in effective Instagram marketing so you must have the resources and skills to produce photos and videos that will stir the interest of your target audience.

Remember, Instagram is predominantly a photo-sharing social media channel, so your content should be designed to fit this model. Hence, you might need to redesign your content from the ground up and make sure that your brand can still convey the right message without using too much text. Do you have the skills to comply with this requirement? If not, you may need to hire an Instagram marketer or outsource the job to an online marketing agency.

Aside from the quality of content, you should also consider quantity. You must regularly post content that asks for comments from your followers. On average, you should aim share 1-2 posts every day. Don't go beyond this limit as your followers may unfollow you for posting too often, especially if your posts are all about products.

Instagram Should Not Be Your Only Channel for Online Marketing

While Instagram can provide amazing benefits for your online marketing efforts, it should only be part of a greater marketing mix.

For example, you should not expect a big surge of online traffic from Instagram because the platform is not designed for that. Instagram engagement is more about likes and comments and not clickthroughs mainly because you can't include links to your posts. You can only direct your followers to your website on your account biography.

If you want to increase clickthroughs, you should definitely include other online marketing strategies such as Search Engine Optimization and Facebook Marketing.

Also remember that just like Facebook, Instagram is also a "Pay-to-Play" platform. This is in fact among the biggest misconceptions businesses often have. Some marketers who are not familiar with the platform think that all of their followers will see their posts. Instagram's algorithm puts a limit on the number of followers who can see your content. If you want your posts to reach everyone, you have to pay for the privilege. Without boosting your post as an advertisement, only a small percentage of your followers may engage in your content.

Hence, in considering Instagram as a marketing channel for your brand, you should also consider the amount you're willing to invest in this platform.

In summary, you should consider the following factors to determine if Instagram is right for your business:

Age Demographics of your target audience (Instagrammers are between 18 and 35 years old)

Your target audience's device preference (Instagram is a mobile app)

The nature or industry of your brand (Successful brands on Instagram are mainly related to food, drinks, health, beauty, retail, and lifestyle)

Your skills and resources to regularly produce engaging content

Your marketing mix and overall online marketing strategy

Once you have determined that your brand can take advantage of Instagram, the next step is to define your target audience and make sure that your brand is properly aligned with your customers and not the other way around.

Chapter 2: How To Perfectly Set Up Your Instagram Business Account For Marketing

Now the first thing after creating your profile picture will be to establish your Instagram profile so that you can start building your impact. The first thing that you should do before setting up your Instagram account is to download the app. In case you don't have it, the app is free to download both on Android devices and iOS devices. You can download the app on both Windows 8 phone, or later. If you have an Android device, then you can download the app through the Google Play store. Instead, if you have an iOS device such as an iPhone or an iPad, then you can download the app through the App Store.

You can also access the Google Play Store through your computer or through your mobile device. Now, if you're using a Windows phone, then you can download the app through your Windows Phone Store. Now even though you can install the app on your laptop, you can only share videos and photos from your mobile devices, so once you click on the install button from Google Play, you should wait for the app to download. Once the app is downloaded tap on it to open it. Once you have done that, then you need to create your account.

So, once you open the app, tap sign up, then you'll be provided with an option to sign up using Facebook to log into your account or with your email. Choose the email option, then you'll be provided with a space to enter your e-mail address, then you'll also be provided with a space to enter your username and your password. Enter your username and your password, then fill out your profile, and then once you are done, click on the done button. If you registered with Facebook, then you'll be prompted to log into your Facebook account and sign in through there. If you are creating your Instagram account with your laptop, then you should click on the Instagram website and once you have opened it, then click on the sign-up button. Make sure that you enter your email address correctly, and choose an email that you can access and a password that you can easily remember.

Now before we continue just to let you know that as you are creating your Instagram account, you are creating an Instagram account for your followers, you want them to know what is in for them. As they tap that follow button, you want them to be converted from followers into customers, into the client, and from followers into followers of your other project, and followers of your other account, which is the main goal. You don't just want them to remain followers, you want them to funnel them down your channel.

So, once you have identified your ideal customers and found your target audience, you want them to follow you. So, the best way to do that is by giving them something that they need or what they want. You should remember that your account should help them convince them that you have what they want and need. It is not about you, but it's about your audience. So, whatever you are creating should be about your audience.

If you are promoting yourself at your personal brand, then you can display yourself but you have to do that in a very strategic way. You have to do that in a way that communicates the type of person that you are. You have to do that in a way that communicates the type of person that you are. For instance, if you are hoping to attract people that need to travel because you like to travel a lot, then you should focus on your travel life and not on your social life or not on your personal relationship life. So, you have to think about this when creating your Username, your profile, and your bio. Your profile name and your username should display the niche that you are.

If you are a personal brand, then you can use your real name, but in addition to that, you can put a globe and a plane emoji at the end of your profile name that is if you are into travel so that people will know that just from seeing you on the list of suggestions of followers. They will know that you are into travel without even clicking through to your profile, so you should have a very intentional plan for your profile and for your website. If you have a blog, then you should link the blog to the front page of your profile. And also, with each post that you make, you should try to put the link of your website so that people be able to click through to your website. This will give people a very good idea about the type of travel topics that you talk about and the type of traveler that you are.

So on your bio link will entice the target audience to read your blog and persuade them to check out the type of contents that you are creating, so that when your target audience click the link and arrive on your page, they will see something that will inspire, help them and interest them and they will probably follow you. Also, you want to be picky about each content that you create. Only post content that you know that your ideal audience will want to see. If you're a travel account, then don't post content about your pets or your midnight party. People like to guide their feed so even an off-topic content might turn them off and they might not follow you.

Optimize your Instagram Profile

The next one is to optimize your Instagram profile. Your Instagram profile should be optimized in a way to engage in brand marketing. You can optimize your Instagram profile in numerous ways. You must be very careful when trying to select a strategy for your brand. Because every strategy must be driven by very specific objectives, because while some profile optimization may work for you, it might not work for others and why some might work for others, it might not work for your brand.

There are so many reasons behind this, and it is a mystery so it is therefore recommended that you carry out a very well-thought-out feasible and comprehensive study so that you'll be able to know the tactics that will yield the results that you want to achieve with your brand. Include various ways including determining the most appropriate image size for your brand, the number of characters or words that will fit perfectly with your promotional messages and post. You need all these things to be able to get the most out of your online marketing.

If you do this appropriately, then you stand the chance of succeeding in your marketing efforts on your Instagram page.

The Not Easy Choice of the Username

The next one is to choose a name, a username, a profile picture and much more that will attract customers. You want to choose a recognizable and unique username, which is one of the most important aspects of your Instagram profile. A good username will allow people to be able to identify you. So, you need to choose a username that is memorial, a username that is recognizable, and a unique username. There are many factors to consider when choosing a username and one of those factors is the length of the username.

Short User Name

Basically, the shorter your username is, the better it is much easier for people to type it the shorter username and search it out and for them to even remember it out. Also, a shorter username will look cleaner. A shorter username will allow more people to be able to engage with you. If you have a long username, then it will be difficult for people to be able to mention you in a comment or in a post so they will likely not even bother to mention you.

The Readability

Another factor to consider is readability. It is very easy to have a short username because it'll be very easy for people to look it out and read it out. If people are going to have to think hard to separate different letters of an unrecognized word, then your username is not going to succeed on Instagram.

The Neatness

The next point to think about his neatness. Now when it comes in neatness, you want the letters of each of your usernames to be close to each other. You can use an underscore to separate the words of your username. An underscore is an easy way to improve the reliability of your username and ensure that it will not be read in the wrong way or it will not be too difficult to separate each word.

The Consistency

The next tip to consider is consistency. It is very important to make sure that all your user names are consistent across all your social media networks so that people be able to remember your niche and they won't have to think hard to remember multiple versions of your username. They will just remember one of the usernames that you used on Twitter or Facebook or YouTube. So, you shouldn't confuse your followers at all no matter which platform you are on and consistency is very important especially when you're sharing a post from one platform to another. For instance, if you are sharing a post from

Facebook to Instagram, then it is good to have one particular username linked to your account.

Easy to Remember

Another thing to consider is if it's easy to remember. people need to be able to remember your username. A username like "the cave" is very easy to remember why username like the "cave 360", is very difficult to remember because it requires digit and the numbers of the digit. Now, unless something is a recognizable part of your business, try to avoid using unnecessary digit or necessary letters on your username. Also, avoid using a middle initial or a random number. Also, if the username that you want to use for your Instagram profile is unavailable, then you should create a version of the username by adding underscore abbreviations. But try to make the username as easy to remember as possible. Only use numbers that make sense and really connect to your brand.

Easy to Pronounce

The next step is easy to pronounce. Now, this tip is very easy to overlook as most people tend to focus on how they are username is. When your username is what will increase its and memorability the way your username looks is what will encourage people to be able to share them on social media or on a podcast. Your username will not be shareable if people find it difficult to pronounce the spelling or to pronounce the word. For instance, if you have the word too in your username, it will be difficult to pronounce it because people can mistake it for 2(TWO). Also, the word tonight might be mistaken for tonight. All these things are the things that will make people not being able to say your username out loud, especially on a podcast.

Correlate with Your Brand

Also try to choose a username that correlates with your business name as much as possible, so that people will be able to find you through your brand name without having your username. People don't need to know your username to be able to find you; that is one thing you have to remember. If your desired username is not available, then try using the word hello or install before it. Many brands and influencers have used it, and it has worked just fine for them.

Take Pictures

The next step is your pictures. You need to put aside any picture that looks over-edited, low-quality or Grey. There is much competition on Instagram that has good edited pictures so if your picture is greyish or Greenish, then people will not want to follow you. If somebody is looking for an account that is into fashion fitness or travel, then they will want an account that has the best photo.

Focus on Your Captions

The next step is your captions. Many niches these days are over-saturated. So, it is very hard to post unique pictures and one way to stand that out of the crowd is to give more or pay more heed to your captions. You can tell a story, and showcase your personality using your captions alone, so do not neglect that opportunity. One good benefit of using the caption is it helps to give your audience something to be able to comment on, and the more the comment on your caption the more the algorithm value.

Complete Properly Your Business Profile in a Marketing Perspective

The next step is to complete your profile. So, you should complete your profile by filling out all the necessary things that you need to fill. Fill out your name and your bio. Make sure that your bio is perfect. Use the name that you know that people will be able to easily recognize. Do not use an obscure phrase or a nickname for your Instagram username. Instead, use an actual name that people will be able to easily used to recognize you.

Use Clever Phrases

Use clever phrases and memorials words in your bio so that people that are visiting your page will be inspired and compelled to follow your recognizable phrases and quotes will leave a huge impact on people's minds. Your bio is also a great place for you to include your current company's hashtag or your brand hashtag. The luggage company supply cool hashtag is well-traveled and the user to promote all their travel-friendly products on Instagram.

Now the luggage company doesn't only include the hashtag in their bio they also include it on all their travel post so that once users see the hashtag, then click on the brand profile and then know what the brand is all about. People will now associate the hashtag with the brand. So, the bio is a great place for you to include your hashtags. Also, the bio is one place that Instagram allows you to include clickable links. So you can include the link of a page or a website so that users can click through to your website, but if you include the link of your website in any other place on your Instagram platform, then the users will need to copy and paste the link into their browser.

Add some Controversy in Your Posts

The next one is to add some controversy in your posting. Controversy stories may not be the best way to get traffic but it's undeniable that people do love controversy. Sometimes so on many occasions, controversial news and gossips have been used by digital marketers to draw traffic to their blog website and other social media platforms. Controversy plays a huge role in attracting traffic to their website. Thus, adding a little controversy to your post on Instagram will help to promote your business.

However before, you start using controversial news and gossip, you should use them very well and you must be aware of all the repercussions that might arise by using this strategy. If you overuse controversies and gossips on your Instagram page, then it can harm your promotional effort, because your followers will appreciate that gossip and controversy with your account which is not good for you as a beginner

So, a little controversy and gossip on your Instagram page will help to promote your business and attract traffic to your profile. However, you should not overuse the strategy because it might damage your reputation among your existing audience and customers.

Include Your Company's Location

The next step is to include your company's location in your bio. This is a great tip, especially if you're a beginner on Instagram. You need to be able to provide accurate information about your location on your bio so that your followers will be able to identify it. location is very important to know that many advantages come with leaving the right information about your company's location. When you leave the right information about your company's location, your followers will be able to determine whether they can buy from your business based on their proximity.

With the right information about the location of your company, you will be able to attract the right and relevant audience who will not only like your images but who will also buy you your company's product. This means that you must provide accurate location information on your bio so that you'll be able to attract followers who are close enough to buy what you're offering. Also providing the right information regarding the area that you are in will help you to identify all the competitors that are in your same niche market and with that information, you'll be able to plan how to counter the influence of your competitors in the market.

So, therefore, you must provide the correct information about your location so that your existing and potential customers will know about it. And you will be able to end their trust as well. So, you need to include the location of your company on your bio so that your followers will know where your company is located.

Include a Call to Action

The next one is to use a call to action to drive traffic since you have created and written your bio.

Chapter 3: Your Magic Powers

Every small business out there has to have some kind of magic powers that their 100 loyal customers love.

Your magic power is basically one thing your business is the best at.

"But dude, my business caters to everyone and we're the best at everything we do!"

Stop right there.

That's not true at all.

If you want to compete, then you gotta have a specialty for your business. This doesn't mean that the other parts of your business is bad.

Nope. This only means that you're really really great at this one thing.

For example:

Say you're a "BBQ Guy"

You own a BBQ restaurant and you have a menu like:

Texas BBQ

Mexican BBQ

Whatever kind of BBQ

Other Menus

You don't have to be the TEXAS BBQ GUY or the MEXICAN BBQ guy, you can be the BBQ GUY, but at the same time, you must have really good sub-menus other than your BBQ.

However, you can also specialize as the MEXICAN BBQ GUY. No one's stopping you from doing this.

The key is to know what you're good at and focus at it.

Once you have your magic powers, you can start focusing your marketing efforts with it in mind.

You don't have to promote that specific products every time, but it will be the cornerstone of your brand.

For example:

KFC

They have lots of other products but their main draw is their fried chicken.

Some Plumber Here in my Town

If you only have one product, then you have to make it unique.

A plumber in my town has a 30 for 1 deal.

He'll be there in 30 minutes and he'll fix it in an hour.

Obviously, he knows whether he can fix it or not in time even before he agrees with the deal.

Cinnabon

Cinnabon's main product is cinnamon rolls.

How about you?

What is your magic power?

The Power of Branding

A strong brand separates you from your competition.

Build a strong brand and you'll never go hungry again.

Your customers will automatically come to you and your business will always be their first choice.

So how do you build a brand that people like and people will connect with?

The answer is through STORIES.

Stories are powerful way to persuade and connect with your customers.

And the best thing about Instagram is you can tell these stories via Images and Videos!

How to apply this in your business?

You can tell your story through pictures

Pictures have the ability to convey emotion and stories.

Post a picture of your business when you were just starting out and tell them how grateful you are to your customers, tell them that you were able to do all of these because of them.

A history wall

I remember when I was eating at my local KFC. I saw these "history wall" and I was able to feel that sense of connection. I don't know if it's just me or not. But the point is, it may help your build a brand for your business.

Share customer testimonials

Part of your story is how you make your customers happy. Take a picture of them while they are on your business establishment and put a quote of their testimonial on the picture.

They are not telling a story but a picture of them on your establishment does convey a story of "Hey, my customers love my business and they go here every time they need my service"

Videos

You can also shoot 30-60 second testimonials and share them on Instagram.

Exercise/Action Steps:

Take a picture of your current customers while they are at your business

Always ask for feedback and testimonials

Write your own story. Answer these questions to formulate your own Home town boy makes good story.

Plus, answer these additional questions.

A. Why did I start the business aside from monetary reasons?

B. Why do I love my business?

C. What are the things I have to go through before making this business a success?

D. What can I consider the small failures and small wins for my business?

E. Write your biggest breakthrough. A certain experience or happening when it all changes for your business.

Chapter 4: What Social Media Can Do For Your Business

Social media is a rapidly growing arena for everything from the posting of videos to car sales, so it should come as no surprise that big business is growing on there, too. However, what can it actually do to help grow your business?

Before selling any product, you have to get your name out there and spread the word of your new social media presence. By adding links to your social media accounts on your company website, you are encouraging people to follow you online in order to get the most up to date information as soon as you release it. When you put your company website on your social media profile, it gives your clients a way to go directly to your website. This will allow your customers to contact your company for more information, and it is more likely to create online buyers.

Social media is the main way that companies are beginning to show involvement with their customers and community by promoting events they are sponsoring or releasing news to their clients. Real-time communication has become extremely important for customer satisfaction in today's businesses. People don't want to wait for answers to their questions or for help resolving any issue they might have. With social media, people have direct access to comments and post feedback for companies, making any kind of wait-time for results obsolete.

Press releases are a thing of the past and take more time to be processed out to customers. By using social media, your company is able to deliver news and updates to clients in real time, while also allowing them to share the news with others and encouraging a faster spread of communication. By letting customers share your company's posts and information, it also allows new people to follow your company page and learn more about your business.

Businesses are turning to Instagram and Facebook, among other social media platforms, to better communicate with their customers and spread the word about their business and future plans. To go about doing this, companies first have to understand the best ways to create brand awareness online and how to draw in new followers.

Building a successful online following will take time. However, there are techniques and skills that will help you build an online following and create a popular social media site, while still promoting your business and keeping in contact with your customers.

The Basics of Brand Awareness

Building brand awareness isn't going to happen overnight, and it won't come from pushing online sales and marketing campaigns on people you don't know. Most of the time, brand awareness actually comes from the process of developing relationships with your customers. Most customers seek an interpersonal relationship with companies from which they plan to purchase.

Think about it in terms of buying a car. If you walk into a car dealership and the salesperson acts aloof while giving you a cut-and-dried spiel about the car, you might feel like the personal aspect of the exchange is a little closed off. However, if the representative you're working with is friendly and shares stories with you, you feel a connection with that person and begin developing trust in them and in the company. Social media essentially works the same way when it comes to brand awareness. You don't have to constantly post about the company and what is happening, but you could post something that your customers relate to, or share something funny to help lighten the mood and develop trust with your customers. Building a relationship with a company is one of the biggest aspects when it comes to return customers. More often than not, people that feel welcomed in a place of business, instead of targeted by sales associates, are going to return for that same experience again. It's human nature to dislike being targeted when it comes to sales. It's frustrating and annoying to have people popping up all around you and trying to force products on you when you aren't even shopping for those items.

How do you effectively get around that issue but still market to your customers? You want to create advertisements that are fun and easygoing. While they do capture the attention of Instagram users, it won't feel like a sales tactics is being shoved down their throats. It gives them the option to scroll past the ad or click to learn more. The Instagram algorithm, which we will review later, notes how long someone looks at a post. So, when you have more people looking at your advertisements and social media posts, it creates more of the same type of post on their page to hold their attention for longer. More attention per post is the main goal of the Instagram algorithm, and shoppers work to its advantage.

Social media has become such a prominent part of a business that over 50% of brand awareness comes from the company's online sociability. What does it mean to have brand awareness, and how can you go about building up your popularity?

Brand awareness comes down to how well your business can be recognized. Another word that you could connect to awareness is reputation. While you are building your business, you want to develop a positive relationship with your clients early on and build up your reputation with customers as much as possible. Social media can almost be considered the same thing as word of mouth nowadays due to how it facilitates the spread of information and the ability to share opinions online.

In order to create more brand awareness, you should use recognizable hashtags. Hashtags can be clicked on and followed through social media in order to see all the posts on the platform with that hashtag attached. Imagine trying to find a company that works on different online marketing strategies. Customers could go on Instagram and search #marketing. Any pictures attached to that hashtag would come up, and if your company has been tagging its posts with that simple word, you could end up bringing new people to your page.

A new tactic on Instagram is its story mode. Accounts can post videos or pictures to their online story and it only keeps it up there for 24 hours. A story post will notify any of your followers that you have posted to your story so that they know to go look at it. Instagram is more photo-based than any other social media platform, so if you want to post videos as well, it's best to keep them short. Videos have the capability to share more information at a faster rate. It makes the time that a user is watching more valuable, and, typically, more information can be provided in the same amount of time used to stop and read a caption. So, if people are scrolling through their feeds and a video starts playing, they might stop to see what it's about.

You're not playing a movie; just give your followers a taste of what you're trying to show. By not giving them the entire picture upfront, they are going to want to come to your page in order to get more information about the product or service that you are selling. Big business companies like Apple and Microsoft never even say their company name in any commercial. Why? People know their products and their company. You want to be able to build your company up online to where, when people see your logo, they instantly know the company that is writing that message. Brand awareness also comes with brand trust, which leads to people buying your product and you gaining a following. In order to get more people to follow your page and like your photos, interaction is key. The more you interact with people following your account, the more you are going to build the following that you need.

Gaining Followers Online

In order to get your business out there on social media, you are going to want people to share your post to their page as gain more attraction to your business page. In order for people to share your posts, however, you are going to need to build a following on your page first.

There have been several studies done on social media marketing to see how popularity works on the web. There are certain styles of pictures and promotion tactics that followers are drawn to more than others. However, the main way to get new followers and attract attention to your page is through hashtags. While there is a limited number of hashtags that can be added to each photo, 30 to be exact, research shows that, ideally, you want to have anywhere from 8 to 10 hashtags attached to the post. Overwhelming your post with an assortment of hashtags will not only be distracting for the customer viewing the post, but will also make your business appear tacky and unorganized. You shouldn't need to post any more than 10 in order to get your main points across. Hashtags are meant to be used as filters to allow users to find more relatable and interesting content. They are also used to make online connections from photos to businesses and people alike in order to connect them through similarities. Two entirely different people could post pictures with #sixflags on them, but they can connect through sharing similar experiences with the rest of the world while also marketing the excitement and enjoyment that Six Flags can provide.

When people are able to connect with one another based on similar experiences and desires, it creates a web of communication that the Internet hub has been building for years. Instagram used to be a social outlet only and wasn't originally designed to be a shopping platform for internet marketers. Nowadays, people have instant access to everything and are able to review companies and their standard of care for customers within a few short clicks. Building a following online is the best way to prevent people from searching for negative aspects of your company. By providing excellent customer service and online assistance to people through the different social media platforms, you will create a positive spike in the algorithm data. Your customers will continue to follow and promote you through commenting on and sharing your posts.

What type of hashtags should you be adding to your social posts? According to Ana Gotter, writer for the Shopify Blogs, there are six categories of hashtags that people are looking at and that you should focus on for your posts:

Branded Hashtags — First, you have your branded hashtags, which are used to promote your company name. You should use these on most of your posts, especially when posting specifically about something that your company is doing. It creates brand recognition, and whenever someone uses your product or attends an event for your company, you should encourage them to use the hashtag as well. This will help spread brand awareness and give your company the opportunity to reach a broader spectrum of followers.

Contest Hashtags — Next, you have contest hashtags, which are rather easy to understand. They are used to promote any contests or promotional giveaways that your company sponsors. You can pair these easily with the name of your company to create a gateway for followers to get to your page for more information.

General Hashtags — General hashtags are the most diverse and hit the widest spread of audience. Sometimes, they even include the name of the social media site they are on, creating internal marketing for the site itself. For example, general hashtags can range anywhere from #petsofinstagram to #ilovemyjob. The generality of the topic allows people to post from all different categories and still fall under that hashtag, as well as find similar posts and photos that draw their interest.

Niche-Specific Hashtags — Niche-specific hashtags revolve around a specific topic. You will often see these on things such as products designed after pop culture. You might see advertisements for things like **Doctor Who** products designed after the hit TV show, or **Harry Potter** or **The Hobbit** jewelry or accessories that are replicas or similar to designs from the movies. When people look at the hashtags #doctorwho or #harrypotter and find a product related to the topic of interest, they will more than likely consider buying it.

Timely Hashtags — Timely hashtags have to do with the "now" topics and usually incorporate holidays or special events that are going on. You might have hashtags like #valentines2019 or #christmasvacation, or even smaller holidays such as #nationalbestfriendday, which may be a trending topic for that moment.

Entertaining Hashtags — The entertaining hashtags are usually things like #toobadsosad or #overit which are more attention-grabbing and funnier. Usually, they are somewhat relevant to the topic, but might not be directly related. Using #overit could be on a post about a stressful work day and being ready to go to bed and start fresh the next day. Even though the post itself doesn't specifically say anything about being "over it," the topic and statement both align with the post.

You should pick out a series of hashtags that best sums up your post and pictures in order to keep things fresh. You should also avoid using the exact same hashtags for every single post. You want to be able to diversify your posts in order to reach different people online and have a wider span of people learning about your company and your promotions. The only hashtag that you should use every time is your branded hashtag, and even then, you should only use it on posts promoting your business. If you are sharing someone else's post or another company post, give them credit by adding their hashtag and commenting on either what they are doing or what you hope to accomplish together.

When you use hashtags, you are able to look at what other people have posted associated with those hashtags as well. You should take note of the other hashtags they use on their posts so that you can add them to your list of potential ones to use in the future, or to research and see what people are saying on the topic. For example, while you may have used #marketing, you might notice that, on another user's post, they used #marketing and #publicrelations. You can then look into the hashtag for public relations and see where that takes you. You want to keep your business in the same category as what you are posting about, and you don't want to use random tags just to bring attention to the post. This will appear unprofessional and distasteful in the eyes of other business professionals who are looking at your posts.

Hashtags are a great way to find new topics for discussion as well. For example, if your business is all about marketing, you may have never thought about advertising for public relations. Being able to expand into different markets is much easier with social media because it creates connections through millions of different people across a multitude of topics.

Then, you have the Instagram storyboard. At one point you were only able to put up one story, all in a single cycle, for people to watch through. However, now there is a way that you can actually make multiple different stories for different categories and attach them to your profile. Instagram decided to call these new stories "highlights," and the platform allows them to stay on your profile for longer than the original 24 hours. Posting highlights creates a way for your followers to watch certain videos without having to view all of them. Let's say your company is having a company retreat and you want to create a story just for that specific day. You can title it "2019 Retreat" and then post only stories involving that retreat's activities and experiences for people to watch. They won't have to filter through any other story highlight information you have posted if it isn't relevant to what they're looking for.

So, now that you have built your page and developed a line of hashtags that work best for your brand, it's time to move on to creating your marketing campaign to get people to your website and buying your products. Make sure you are following other people in the industry to see what they are posting or what promotional activities they are running in order to get a better idea of how you can improve your own company's social media presence. It's a common misconception that watching your rival companies is cheating. Think about how often cell phone companies play cat and mouse with one another over the newest trends and technology: bigger screens, better headphones, more wireless capabilities. By watching what other companies do, you are able to hone in what people are expecting to get from the business. You can create your own version of the plan that other companies are developing because, at the end of the day, customers will choose the one that gives them the most positive feeling. Plus, it's good to be cordial with competing companies. Beyond it being a decent thing to do, friendly competition is a great way to get people interested in what's happening online.

For example, think back to when Wendy's and McDonald's had online Twitter comments going back and forth. It took the internet by storm and was reposted all over the different social media platforms. People were sharing and talking about it, which encouraged other companies to get involved online in the clapback marketing comments. All of the competition was promoting their food items, and talking about the cooking styles of the fast food restaurants and the deals they had going on. While it was funny and attention-grabbing, people were also spreading the word that the chicken nuggets at Wendy's were more expensive but fresher than those at McDonald's. Your competition isn't your enemy, and it could be good to use some of their strategies.

Following your opposing companies also allows you to see what types of marketing strategies they use to bring in their customers. This can help you develop your plans to be more effective in the future. As people use different businesses, they are going to like certain aspects about one and other things about another. The more research that you conduct as you study up on customers that search through similar hashtags, the more you will notice a trend in the types of business styles they like and the environment they are looking for when they choose a business to work with. This allows you to add to and change your marketing strategy to suit more people's wants when it comes to picking a company.

You can search through different hashtags on Instagram, which allows you to find content that is related to what you are trying to post. It could help you find inspiration on what to post while also allowing you to see what others are currently talking about in the market, or what they are looking to achieve from the market. You may also find other businesses that you can work with, depending on the hashtags that they have attached to their post.

By following different companies and individuals, you are getting a better assessment of what is going on in the industry, and how to use it to your advantage when you begin a new marketing campaign. Gaining followers isn't an overnight project, nor is it a one-time effort. Your company should constantly be striving to increase its online following on all social media platforms by encouraging followers of one platform to like and follow you on the other platforms as well. If you have Instagram followers who haven't liked your Facebook page yet, then you now have the opportunity to gain followers on that platform as well.

Followers begin to like and comment based on the content of the posts, but they can always search through hashtags to find your company. When you begin posting regularly, make sure you include different types of engaging posts for them to read and think about. Otherwise, they might unfollow you to stop clogging their feed. Make sure your posts are relevant to your followers and the projects they are working on or looking to begin on in the near future. For example, if you see a company looking to expand into a new market, you can send them a message online and get on their radar early. You might not get anywhere with it right away, but by being in the background and following them online as they develop the marketing side of their business further, you can continue to offer help along the way in order to keep their mind drawn back to your company if they need assistance. Build your network in any way you can. You probably won't know all your followers, but interacting with them and showing interest in the things that they do will help make your page successful online.

Chapter 5: How To Make Your Instagram Posts Stand Out From The Competition

Competition is vital in every area of life, and Instagram is not exempted. Even if you believe you have no competition, the truth is that some other individual out there is offering the same service as you. So never underestimate the requirements of individuals as they are the same in all aspects of the globe.

So if you are the only one providing a service in a specific region, remember to look for likely competitors around you or in other countries aside from yours. But how can you determine what your competition is doing on social media, specifically Instagram? How do you learn about their behaviors or strategies? Are these answers even essential to you?

Put simply; the answer is yes. You should have an interest in all of these details and understand each of them so you can use the results you attain to build your page on Instagram. In this chapter, you will be learning how to spy on your competition regardless of where they are situated.

 Simply put, you have to learn about your opponent if you want to do better than them. It is also a means of getting inspiration and ideas for how you can promote your brand and grow it. Below are a few ways ethically spying on your competitors can assist you:

Learn where they excel and where they don't: By spying on your Instagram competitors, you will be able to learn the areas they are excelling in and how you can do better from them. Also, by learning the areas they have no success, you will be able to pick lessons from their errors and ensure you don't do the same things.

Find out the kind of content they are sharing: By spying, you will learn if your competition has better content than you, or if they are getting more engagement on Instagram than you do. Then, you can learn about the kind of content to provide and which to stay away from for the best engagement.

Factors that affect the visibility of your posts

The visibility of your Instagram posts is determined by Instagram's algorithm. This algorithm combines mystery with ingenuity. The algorithm is responsible for the Facebook's showing of only the best content to Facebook users.

Engagement

Engagement refers to the degree of popularity of your posts. It is known that a post with a high degree of popularity will have better engagement than one with lower popularity. That explains the connection between the engagement and popularity of a post.

According to the CEO and founder of the popular social media analytics site Social Media Examiner, Michael Stelzner says that whenever you publish a post on behalf of your brand or yourself, the algorithm is designed to show the published post to a section of the target audience. The goal is to see the sample audience's reaction to the post in order to determine how far the post should go. If the response is impressive, it will be shown to the public. Otherwise, if the response is not encouraging, the post will be limited to the sample audience. What is the implication?

Any of you who post with a higher engagement has a better chance at ranking higher on your feed than those with lower engagement. Some of the factors that are considered as parts of engagement include video views, likes, share, comments, story views, saves, and live videos.

Relevance

Your ranking is not determined by your posts alone; it takes another factor into consideration: the relevance your post has to your audience. Why is this important?

When launching the Instagram algorithmic timeline, the social media site announced that importance will be attached to relevance when showing content. So, you will be fed with the posts that you are interested in before any other post.

Tips to make your posts stand out

Instagram marketing works, which is why you can expect tons of other brand similar to yours using Instagram to compete for people's attention. And because of that, each year, it gets harder and harder to increase engagement. That doesn't mean, though, that it's impossible to make the most of your posts. In this section, we offer you a few ways you can take your Instagram strategy to another level and get maximum engagement on your Instagram posts.

Optimize Instagram Story Posts

There are several ways you can optimize every Instagram story that you publish, and one of them is by using location and hashtag stickers. When Instagram Stories first came out, it only allowed users to share them with their own followers. After several updates, stories you post are now searchable both by hashtag and location. This means anyone can now see your stories.

Another way you can optimize Instagram Stories is by adding links to them. By adding a link, you can lead people wherever you want them to go, such as your blog, to a landing page in your main website, to an affiliate page, or to your email list.

Maximize Your Captions

Sometimes, one-liners are simply not enough. Talk as much as you can about your brand through your captions to keep your followers informed. Writing a lengthy caption directly on Instagram is easier said than done, however. The caption box isn't just user-friendly enough for you to edit captions quickly and easily. But thank goodness there are now Instagram schedule apps that let you write, review, and edit captions with ease. Some of these apps, such as Later, even let you save your post with your caption and edit it at a later time.

Make Use of Instagram Stories Stickers

The Instagram Stories feature doesn't only let you share information. More importantly, it lets you converse with your followers, which is crucial if you want them to be constantly engaged and connected to you. One of the easiest ways you can do that is by taking advantage of Instagram Stories stickers.

Instagram Stickers can be incorporated to both image and video stories. Some of these are clickable, some are animated, while others allow your followers to directly interact with your story. Stickers make Instagram posts, particularly stories, more interesting, and this increases the chance of users interacting with your posts. The sticker that you want to use more often are those that let users engage directly with your story, two of which are the Question sticker and the Poll & Vote sticker.

Share More About Your Brand

Instagram is not only a place where you can post pictures of your products hoping people would buy them. More importantly, it's a place where you can share your passion with the world, let people know why your business exists, and who the people are behind the company. That said, you can increase engagement on your posts by sharing more details about your company, like sharing when you're hiring new staff or ideas you have about future products or improvements on current ones.

Spice Up Your Posts

Want to see some real returns in your Instagram posts? If you do, then take time to add some element of fun to your photos, videos, or stories. Of course, you want to stay true to your brand's theme and culture, but that doesn't mean you can't spice up things a little bit. One you can do that is by adding memes from time to time.

Pay Attention to DMS and Comments

Replying to your follower's comments and messages may be a simple gesture, but it goes a long way in gaining people's trust and strengthening relationships. The more DMs, comments, likes, and shares your posts receives, the more Instagram will recognize them as high-quality content, and the more likely they will be visible to a wider audience.

The goal of paying attention to DMs and comments is not simply for boosting engagement. More importantly, it's to find ways to improve your strategy. More often than not, your followers will leave comments and messages both with positive and negative feedback. Use these feedback, whether positive or negative, as a means to enhance your products and services.

Partner with an Influencer

Finally, you'd want to collaborate with an influencer if you are to see any increase in user engagement. Just because a person is famous and has a large following doesn't necessarily mean that he or she is the right person to partner with. The keyword is "like-minded."

Optimize Instagram Story Posts

There are several ways you can optimize every Instagram story that you publish, and one of them is by using location and hashtag stickers. When Instagram Stories first came out, it only allowed users to share them with their own followers. After several updates, stories you post are now searchable both by hashtag and location.

This means anyone can now see your stories.

Another way you can optimize Instagram Stories is by adding links to them. By adding a link, you can lead people wherever you want them to go, such as your blog, to a landing page in your main website, to an affiliate page, or to your email list.

Schedule Your Stories

One way to find out what specific times of the day your followers are active and viewing your Instagram posts the most is through Instagram Insights. It's an analytical tool that provides you with crucial data on the demographics and actions of your followers, as well as the performance of your posts. Within this feature, you will dig a host of information on your profile's performance, including the days and hours your followers are active the most. Knowing when the best time is to post your stories lets you prepare them in advance and schedule them for posting later at the most optimized times.

Share More About Your Brand

There's a universal rule in business that states that people will only transact with those whom they can trust. In short, relationship matters. One way you can form and strengthen your brand's relationship with your audience is by being transparent to them. That could mean opening up more about your business. And if there's one place you can do that, it's on Instagram.

Instagram is not only a place where you can post pictures of your products hoping people would buy them. More importantly, it's a place where you can share your passion with the world, let people know why your business exists, and who the people are behind the company. That said, you can increase engagement on your posts by sharing more details about your company, like sharing when you're hiring new staff or ideas you have about future products or improvements on current ones.

Have A Strong Hashtag Strategy

Hashtags rocketed to fame on Twitter, and now they're found on almost all social media platform. They seem have been taken for granted over the past years, but hashtags are more than just words you use to label your messages. Hashtags are like a compass that point people to your content. Understanding which hashtags to use to drive more people to your posts is the key to increasing your user engagement on Instagram.

Chapter 6: Strategies In Engaging With Your Audience

As you can tell from the previous chapter, uploading and sharing photos or videos on Instagram shouldn't be taken lightly if you are running your account as a business or influencer. But the work doesn't stop there! In order to make your content more effective, you need to make engagement with every post you make and to make posts that will initiate engagement.

When it comes to any social networking, engagement is the key. If you want to improve your presence and attract more followers, then this is a practice you need to master. So, in this chapter, we are focusing on the strategies you can follow to engage with your audience.

Leaving Comments on Brand That Are Within Your Niche

Let's start this chapter by talking about making engagement on other pages within your niche. Yes, you can make engagement outside your territory as long as the account or the post you are leaving a comment on is still within your niche.

When you leave a comment, make sure to add a personal touch by using the name of the owner of the account (Usually, it is located on their bio page, if not, use their username). Choose to leave the comments on accounts with the highest number of following. This is because posts from those accounts are more likely to be seen by many more users. You can also interact with other comments, as long as you're not claiming to be associated with the owner of the account.

When leaving a comment, avoid leaving one-word or just emoji comments. Make sure to read the post and leave valuable comments – it could be questions or some sort of appreciation. Make sure to not always leave the same comment or else, you might get reported as spam, which can leave your account banned.

3.1 How to Respond to Comments on Your Content

Responding to comments left in your content is as important as writing captions on your posts – it does wonder when it comes to the algorithm. Posts with many comments from different people are pushed up by Instagram.

Along with the Instagram algorithm, responding to the comments builds some sort of connection between you and your existing and potential followers. This can generate a positive impact on how they see your brand. These people are likely to feel appreciated and their loyalty to your brand will be stronger.

Here are some tips you can follow when it comes to responding to the comments being left on your posts:

Positive Feedback and Compliments

Getting positive feedback on your post is extremely good for your brand. For many, they would just tap the heart button to show that they like the comment and then move on with their day. There's nothing bad with that, but if you take your time to express gratitude, they will appreciate it more and they will be more than happy to leave you more comments in the future.

So, if you want to make someone appreciated for simply leaving a nice comment on your post, respond to it nicely. A simple "thank you" along with smiling emoji would make them feel like you are one of their friends and not some snob influencer.

Emoji-Only or Single-Word Comments

When someone left this kind of comment, you don't necessarily have to respond to them. But, if you're feeling gracious, as a simple "thank you" or tapping on the heart icon to like the comments would be enough.

Rude or Negative Feedback

Unfortunately, many people still find the need to say something bad on the internet. Instead of expressing their disappointment in a better manner, they choose to lash out and leave hateful comments. When this happens, you can handle this by letting it go and flagging the comment as abusive content.

Remember that it's important for you to keep a good positive image of you for your brand, and engaging with these kinds of people will not help your brand grow, instead, it might even dent it.

As for negative feedback or complaints on your product or service, always keep your professionalism by responding nicely, even if they are cussing – they might not be happy with your service that's why they are angry, and that's okay. Ask them to send you a Direct Message so you can discuss the problem privately. Always keep your calm and don't fight negative comments with aggression. If you need some time to think of what to reply, that's even better. Take your time – take a deep breathe and respond with respect.

Questions

Most of the time, people would ask inquiries about your products, services, or promotions you announced on your Instagram post. You have to be quick in responding to this kind of questions as they might actually want to make transactions with you.

If you want to save some time and actually reply to your potential clients quickly, then you may want to prepare templated answers to the most commonly asked questions. For example, they might ask how they can contact you, type a response to this question on your Notes app and save it. Then when someone asks the same question, you can simply copy that and paste to the comment as a reply. You'll save so much time!

If the question happens to require a longer answer, then encourage the user to send you a Direct Message. Or better yet, send them a message directly, and then reply to their comment saying that you responded to their inquiry via direct message.

Spam and Tags/Mentions

Unfortunately, Instagram still doesn't have full control over spam accounts, and any public Instagram account probably has experienced being mentioned by a spam account. You can simply delete the comment if you don't want them on your post and then report them to Instagram. It's easy to tell whether or not an account is a spam account. The first sign is that they have only a single or no post. They also usually use pictures of sexy women in skimpy clothes or bikini.

As much as it is crucial to update your Instagram account with new posts in order to gain more followers, it's also important to constantly check back into those posts and respond to the comments as soon as possible. This will keep the engagement going. This delivers a positive message to your followers and will push you up on top of the Instagram algorithm. By keeping your engagement game strong, you are working your business' way to the top.

3.2 How to Run a Contest on Instagram

One of the most effective ways to attract new followers and brand recognition is through running a contest on your Instagram. Seriously, if done correctly, you can gain at least 1000 new followers by the end of the contest period.

But is it really worth it? What if you're just starting out on your business? Keep on reading.

3.2.1 Reasons to Run a Contest

Well, no matter how new or old you are in this scene, the answer would always be a YES! Here are some reasons why you should consider running a contest on your Instagram account:

Raise Brand Awareness Through the Platform

In social media, visibility is EVERYTHING. And there's no doubt that running an Instagram contest is one of the fastest ways to get your name out there! Who doesn't love winning free stuff? Your followers will have no problem tagging their friends and family just to have a higher chance to win your contest.

And with this tagging, the ultimate domino effect will take place. Before you know it, everyone who has been tagged will also start tagging and the newly tagged ones will do the same thing and the same thing will happen over and over. And of course, those people tagged and are tagging are likely to follow you to get a track of who's going to win.

Boost the Engagement

When running a contest, get ready to receive tons of notification – it will blow up your phone. You will get flooded with likes and comments. But the Instagram algorithm will love you because of this! You will be shown to more people on Instagram that it thinks will be interested in your contest.

Drive New Followers

If you want guaranteed new followers, then run a contest that requires the participant to follow you before they gain entry to the contest. But then again, even without requiring this, they are still likely to follow you because they want to keep updated with who's going to win in the contest.

3.2.2 Different Types of Contests You Can Run on Instagram

Okay, so by now you've probably convinced that running a contest on Instagram is a brilliant idea. Now let's talk about the different types of contests you can have.

Photo Challenge Contest

This is one of the most popular types of Instagram contests. This involved making participants to upload photos on their account, tagging you, and using specific hashtags for that contest. You can also get them to mention your name in the caption and tagging other friends. This is a good contest that brings domino effect – now that you are mentioned in their post, your name and contest are getting exposure.

Repost-to-Win Contest

Just like the photo uploading contest, this one also involves requiring your followers to post pictures on their personal accounts but in this case, they have to take a screenshot of a specific photo you want them to upload. This photo usually includes your branding as well as the contest details in order for other people to see what's going on. Again, don't forget to require them adding specific hashtags and to tag you.

Like-to-Win Contest

This is the easiest contest to run, and probably the one that gets most participants. This might not get you a lot of new followers but it boosts your place in the algorithm game, more importantly, you're making many of your followers happy.

Comment-to-Win Contest

Like the previous one mentioned, this one is many people's favorite because it requires a minimal effort – just to leave a comment on your post. This can be as simple as asking what they love about your product or service or about something else relevant to your niche or something more creative like giving a caption to your photo. There should be endless ideas! Make sure to limit them to one comment per account, otherwise, your post might get flooded with comments from a single user.

Tag-to-Win Contest

This is something becoming the most popular Instagram contest today. In this contest, the users that want to join are required to tag some of their friends (usually 3 to 5 friends who are on Instagram) and convince them to join as well and follow your page. And before you know it, you're gaining new followers and more engagement.

Follow-Me Contest

Now, the last but not the least is the simple follow-me contest, which definitely is the best way to gain new followers and of course, boost your brand awareness. You can do a combination of any methods of any of the contests mentioned above like having to tag other people, liking your post, or commenting on it, along with having to follow you. Using a mixture of the entry methods above PLUS requiring anyone who wants to enter the contest to follow you. This would be a good way to improve your Instagram account and presence.

3.3 How to Partner with Influencers

Instagram influencers are basically the people who are making it to the top of at social media game. They're considered innovators and experts in this field. They are constantly chosen to be brand advocates due to their strong credibility and wide-ranging reach with a certain audience.

If you want to have leverage in the game, then partner with the right influencer that will truly help your brand. By choosing the right person to partner with, you will have the ability to draw a bigger audience. And to help you do that, here are the important step to finding and reaching out to the right influencer to partner with.

Set a Goal

When partnering with an influencer, it's important to build clear goals or objectives for the strategy you want to execute. Some of the common goals you might have in mind include:

To boost engagement

To increase credibility and brand awareness

To extend the reach of the uploaded content

To increase brand awareness and credibility

To gain more followers

You can set the SMART method in setting your goals.

Specific

Measurable

Attainable

Realistic

Timely

One of the biggest mistakes you can make is reaching out to an influencer and asking them to make a collaboration with you without a proper plan. You'd be super lucky if you ever get a reply! If you want to be more successful, make sure that you are prepared – do homework, and define your SMART goal. It's important that you explain to them clearly what your intentions are and why you are doing it.

For example, if you are running an account with a niche related to cooking, you can collaborate with a chef influencer and show your interest in wanting to post one of their recipes on your account. As you do so, you have to provide them good information on how they can benefit from it. You need to propose them irresistible offers that would make them hard to say no to.

Regardless of what your reason is for asking them to collaborate with you, it's extremely important that you can tell them what you want to happen exactly. So, make sure that in the proposal you are going to write – which we are going to talk further later on – you tell them what you want, how you want it to be done, and how they can benefit from it.

Learn from Existing Brands

For first-timers, the best place to get started is to do research about your competitions and how they work things out. You can also monitor just any account within your niche but outside your demographics. Study the kind of content they post to see which content gain the highest level of engagement.

Generate a Plan of Action

Coming up with a plan of action is the next crucial thing you need to do. When generating a plan of action, you can start with a brief and tangible goal. This will allow you to have a particular target and help the influencer learn further what you really want.

You're the one to decide which goal suits better with your business and marketing tactics. Even though it's very important to have an action plan, you should allow your influencer to do their own thing and use their creativity.

Don't try to control them and limit them in expressing themselves. You want their message to be authentic.

Identify the Best Influencer for Your Brand

When searching for the right influencer for your brand, it's important for you to be aware of the desires, goals, aspirations, and fears your customers share. By making yourself aware of this information, you will easily determine the most influential people for your followers and targeted audience. Keep in mind that influence is not equal to popularity. Remember that followers can be bots and bought – not because someone has a huge following, it doesn't mean that you can benefit from them 100%.

When searching and choosing for influencers, here are three important Rs you need to focus on:

Reach: These stats reveal the size of the audience of the influencers. This will be the number of followers, average likes, and comments.

Resonance: This will tell you how the followers interact with the content of the influencer uploads. This is the number of comments, likes, and shares.

Relevance: This will tell you how relevant their niche is to yours. This would be the hashtags and keywords used whenever the influencer makes a post.

By checking out the influencers' reach, resonance, and relevance, you will be able to know more about their impact on the community and how and if they can truly benefit your brand. Just like a real-life relationship, it's important to make some sort of connection or rapport with them before making any form of deal with them. You can start making connections with influencers by interacting with them as a follower.

Leave nice comments and like their posts, maybe share their contents, then, later on, reach out via DM. By doing this right and in a consistent manner, connecting and collaborating with influencers will be easier.

Build Real Relationships with Influencers

At this point, you should know which influencers you might want to reach out to and what you are going to tell them derived from your goals, what the next question is, and how are you going to approach them. Should you slide them a DM? Should you email them? How about the pitch, how would you compose it?

Here are some tips that can help you put things together

Think like the Influencer

Put yourself in the influencer's shoes. Think of what their priorities are and what their goals could be. The area they are in and what interests them. When collaborating with the influencers that you want, let them know the reason why you are approaching them and how and if they can really make a difference to your campaign.

Show What You Have to Offer

When it comes to offering values, you must also have something to put on the table. If you can benefit from the other brand as well, then you'll have a higher chance to get the collaboration. Otherwise, it's a shoot for the moon, unless you are willing to pay the influencer to do the collaboration. If you are uncertain, there's nothing wrong with asking them what you could do for them and what kind of leverage they may possibly be looking for to make them agree with the collaboration.

You can also send them some of your products as a gift – they can even give your products free reviews (which can also drive you traffic) if they're feeling generous in return for your generosity. But in the end, what you want is to make them agree to collaborate with you.

94

Make Relevant Offers

Keep in mind that the demand of your market is not the only thing that is important, but also what the influencer wants. If your niche aligns with the interests and values of the influencers, they'll be more interested in engaging with your campaign and they'll be more invested in the partnership you are trying to offer.

Keep in mind that the influencers you are reaching out to are also people with hobbies and passion. If you figure out their interests, it's going to be easier for them to figure out how they can contribute to your campaign and get successful results.

By letting the influencers align their passions with your brand, it will generally lead to a more invested partner who is more motivated in promoting your brand and/or the product you are trying to offer.

3.3.1 How to Make the Perfect Pitch for Collaboration

Making the perfect pitch is the key to convincing the influencer to agree to collaborate with you. A pitch is meant to pinpoint the information that is relevant and valuable for the influencer's decision-making.

A pitch should be professionally but lightheartedly written but more importantly, genuine and straight to the point. Here is a template you can follow:

Hi, [Name of the Influencer]!

I am [Your name] from [Your company]. I've been following your account for a while - [Talk about what convinced you to follow them and what you like about what they post].

I am sending this message to you to ask if you'd be interested in partnering with us for a [The concept goes here, e.g. product review, contest, etc.]

We offer [Write what you offer to the influencer here, e.g. monetary payment, free products, etc.]

It's up to you how you want to present the content - your unique outlook is what we are eager to have.

If you're interested, can we set up a call to discuss this further?

I hope to hear from you!

Best,

[Your name]

Of course, you can customize this mail according to your preference. Just make sure you offer relevant, genuine information.

Do the Hard Work

Do the hard work – your influencer is not your staff. As much as possible, you want to make it easy for your new partner to carry out the job. For example, if the influencer needs to know more details about the product involved, get resources ready for them. If you want them to say something more specific about the product, let them know exactly how you want it to be written (this is usually applicable for those who are paid to do the collaboration). They might make some modifications, but it's going to be better for them if they don't have to do it from scratch.

Make a Decision on How the Partnership Works

Again, once you have found the best influencer to collaborate with, you must have an agreement that can benefit both of you. And here are the most important aspects you have to focus on:

Content: Both parties should agree on the type of content that will be created for your brand. This means that even though you agreed that the influencer has the right to say anything he or she wants, it still has to have your approval. For example, you have to make sure that the information being shared is accurate or the link included is written correctly.

Time: Don't forget to set a specific deadline on when you need the content to be published and the influencer must agree to it.

Rights & Ownership: Create an agreement about content usage rights. In general, the content creator (the influencer) has every right to that content, however, they still have to have your permission if they want to share it somewhere else other than their Instagram. They also can't hold ownership of the brand and must declare that it's only a collaboration (only if that's what you want).

Retribution: Clarify the payment method, dates, and amount that you agree to pay even before starting the project. You can always negotiate or even get a free service in exchange for something else – like doing the same thing for them on your own account or free products or services. But then again, if they refuse to accept the offer unless it's paid monetarily, you must respect that. Keep in mind that it took them a lot of time and a lot of hard work before they got to the point where they currently are.

Hashtag use: You have to know that there are different regulations when it comes to sponsored content, and they change all the time. However, it's important that the influencer is using the hashtags #spon or #ad in your campaign. This will tell the people who will see it that the post is a sponsored post.

Chapter 7: Building And Developing Your Profile

When building your Instagram page, you have to make sure to be clear about who you are and what you stand for.

There should be consistency and it should reflect in the posts you make. The posts should be unified in the messages and the overall look. You have to make your posts look uniform, so that if someone goes through 20 posts you can easily know it's yours. If you can do this consistently, you will see your follower count will climb and engagement on your page will increase.

You can pick out about five Instagram accounts that are telling the same visual story you want to tell. The examples will help you draft a branding sample you can use. Whenever you intend to create a post, it will serve as a guide and help you stay in line with the visual story you want your brand to be identified with.

Word Swag - This is an Instagram app that helps you create Instagram images. You can easily select the same font every time. The app has different designs for each font style, so each of your posts will have a different look, but will still be uniform. You can also blur or soften the background image so you can highlight your text.

Add your brand stamp at the bottom of the image or quote that you are posting. Some people believe that when you don't add your brand stamp, the engagement on your page will increase. This is not true, rather it will get you targeted traffic. And as much as you want traffic and hundreds of followers, they should be from your target audience that at the end of the day will be interested in buying your products or services.

There's also a lot of argument whether quotes are more ideal to post than photographs. It totally depends on the niche you are in and what you are offering. If you are not selling a physical product, but selling information or offering online services, posting quote images can work for you. However, if you are a retailer, a fitness trainer, or into beauty services, photographs will do a better job for you. If you still can't decide what to post often, take a look at some Instagram pages in the same niche as yours. Find out if they are uploading quote images or photos and what other content they are posting.

The overall question you should ask yourself is if your brand were a person, how would you want its personality to be described? What is the personality you want associated with your brand? What is the message you want your brand to convey in each post?

Taking time to find the answers for these questions will help you make your decision. The amazing thing about building your own brand is the fact you can mold and build it into whatever you want.

Instagram tools you can use to build your Instagram account

Reels

Instagram also favours accounts who use their tools, so make sure you embrace any of the new features they roll out.

The new feature they recently released and that is trending is Reels, which is similar to Tik Tok. Reels is a series of short videos you upload to your stories or profile . You can do a test run by uploading two videos; a live video and a reel video. I assure you 100% that the reel video will get more views and engagement.

You may be wondering how that is even possible. Well, it's Instagram's latest feature, which means they want more people to use it and know about it. They need you to help them get more people using this new feature, so whenever you use it they tend to give you more exposure and show your post to as many people as possible.

If you need visibility and reach, you shouldn't miss out on using Reels.

IGTV

IGTV is the standalone app of Instagram. It is used for posting longer videos. You can use this to post longer videos for your business, like unveiling a new product for your brand, or a Q&A session for your followers.

The same way you reward your followers for engaging on your page is the same way Instagram will reward when you use their tools.

Hashtags

You can barely do business on Instagram without using hashtags. It's not a smart business move to avoid using hashtags.

Using just one hashtag increases your post engagement by 12%. It is a very effective method for driving organic traffic to your page.

The trick to using hashtags is using tags that will drive specific and quality traffic to your page. Remember, the goal is not just to pull in the crowd, but to bring in a crowd that will be interested in what you have to offer and you will be able to solve their need.

Be specific with the hashtags you use, not just using the ones you see everyone using. Using target hashtags shouldn't stop you from using popular hashtags too. You want the hashtags to be specific, but you have to also make sure it's popular and frequently used. If you use unpopular hashtags, you may not be able to reach out to the audience you are targeting. One strategy is to choose around 10 hashtags that are extremely targeted and don't have as many publications (less than 50k), 10 medium hashtags ((between 100k and 50k publications), and 10 big hashtags (over 100k)

If you are clueless on the hashtags to use, review 10 or more brands that are popular in your niche. Check out all the hashtags they frequently use and start testing them one after the other. Make a master list then start trying out different combinations and variations of the tags. Keep track of all the progress they are making, so you can easily determine the ones that are working for you.

You may find it difficult to try everything at once. Try creating an Instagram post signature, then go on to save it on an online list keeper. You can easily select and paste this way.

The maximum amount of hashtags you are allowed to use is 30. Use them all, as the more hashtags are used in a post the more people it will reach. Avoid repeating hashtags in every post, as this can be detected as spam. Instead, try to mix around 10 or 15 of your tags and choose ones that are related to your post.

Chapter 8: Factors That Have Effect On Instagram

After exploring Instagram, you'll notice that there are factors that affect competitors

—you must keep an eye on your competitors.

There are a number of users who try to reach the same audience that you try to attract to your blog with similar ideas.

You don't just have to know who your competition is, you need to know what they are doing, how they are doing, what they are doing, and how it measures against what you are trying to achieve.

Take note on the different types of strategies your competitors have used, and you see if you can run something similar on your page.

You should always use your competitor's blogs as inspiration to do better. You should never view your competition as "the enemy."

It will lead to breeding unnecessary negativity into the air. Healthy competition is good for any business, and it keeps you on your toes and prevents you from slacking in any aspect.

Star factors

—You want your star factor to be identified. You can start by identifying what you are really good at doing and capitalizing on it.

For example, if you manipulate photos well, concentrate on uploading manipulated photos that you have captured.

You can post your photo in its original and edited version.

This will wow your audience, and they may eagerly anticipate what you have to offer next.

If this is your goal, let photo manipulation be your selling point in the graphic design focus. Let people know you for that.

You can also try to promote your blog in a way that makes your audience feel like you are above the rest.

Trust is paramount in every aspect of life. If you want people to believe in what you have to offer, convince them. If they don't follow your blog, make them feel like they're missing out.

Please note that if you keep fueling posts that lack personality and focus exclusively on promotion, people may end up thinking that your blog is a spam blog.

Originality is key

—This we've established a lot.

One of the best ways to keep Instagram original is to cultivate your blog in such a way that it talks to the followers.

You must have a star factor, which is unique in your blog.

This is your brand.

It must be something that your competitors don't have and work hard to achieve.

You can't afford to accept anything unusual or generic in your blog.

The Instagram algorithm

—A smart programming that determines the order of posts Instagram presents in the feed of any user.

All posts were delivered in sequence in the old days (pre-2016) with your newest posts at the top of your feed.

As Instagram became more popular, this became unmanageable.

The Instagrammer average got far too many posts to see it all.

This meant that a lot of posts were never even viewed, merely because they were way too far down in the feed.

Instagram has changed its algorithm quite a few times over the last few years.

It moved from its chronological feed in 2016, with an effort to best guess the preferences of each of its individual users. You have to take this algorithm into account and really pay attention to the best times of the day to post your photos/videos.

In order to stand out, your content needs to have something that sets you apart from your fellow Instagramers.

This is actually also something you need to think about when planning out your blog.

Chapter 9: The Power Of Hashtags, Liking, And Commenting – And How Not To Get Banned

Now that you have an account and understand how to present your photos, now you have to understand how to share them efficiently with the rest of the Instagram crowd. If you simply post photos and do nothing else... well, your photos won't be seen.

Step 1: The art of the hashtag

If you're at all familiar with Twitter, you have likely heard of the term "hashtag" before. A "hashtag" is another word for the pound key, or: #. What hashtags do is allow photos to be grouped together based on keywords. The hashtag tells Instagram that you're intending that particular photo to be grouped with other photos under the same hashtag.

You want to use hashtags to ensure that people who are interested in topics related to your business can see your photos.

So, if Bob from Bob's Widgets posts a picture, he might write a caption like, "These brand new widgets are seriously beautiful! #newproduct #widgets #newwidgets #widgetsarethebest"

In this example, the photo that Bob has posted will appear linked with the key terms "newproduct" "widgets" "newwidgets" "widgetsarethebest."

You will need to do research into your particular vertical to discover what the best key terms are for you to hashtag. A good way to do this is to check out the successful Instagram feeds of competitors. What are they hashtagging?

Additionally, you'll want to keep abreast of current events and terms. For instance, around the holiday season you may want to start adding hashtags like "Christmas" or "Thanksgiving" or "Chanukah" or so on, so that your photos appear in those feeds, which will be very popular at that time of year.

You can also create your own hashtags. For instance, if Bob is promoting a widget bonanza, he might try #bobswidgetbonanza

Creating your own hashtags is very useful once you've gotten an active Instagram following. Bob might try, "Take a picture of yourself using my widgets and hashtag #bobswidgetbonanza for a chance to win 20% off your next widget purchase!"

Interested customers will take pictures and hashtag to enter the contest. Not only does this up engagement with Bob, but it also will appear in the feeds of persons who are following the contest participants, thus extending Bob's reach. We will discuss more about contests later on in this eBook.

Sending photos out on Instagram with no hashtags is the equal to throwing a message in a bottle out into the ocean. However, it is also possible to overdo it on hashtags. Generally speaking, a good average would be 3-8 hashtags per post. Too much and your posts risk looking too salesy.

Step 2: Learning to love the like

When you are browsing through your Instagram feed (you can find it under the icon that looks like a house), you'll see tons of pictures from people you are following and people that hashtag topics you are interested in and so forth. It is very important to scroll through this and hit the "heart" icon on the posts.

This is a "like." You will be notified when somebody likes your posts, and others will be notified when you like theirs. This is how you start building your community around you.

You may wonder if it's appropriate to like the posts of competitors. After all, it is highly likely that you will see plenty of them appearing in your feed, as they will be promoting the same or similar products as you and thus will be using the same key terms a lot of the time.

The answer to this is yes. Remember that Instagram is a community, not a direct sales platform. You are not trying to outshine your competitors here - rather, you are trying to build community. The more you interact with everybody who is involved in the community built by your hashtag choices, the better your own Instagram presence will be. Interact with everybody - customers, competitors, whomever.

The more you like the posts of others, the more followers you will get and the more than people will like your posts, resulting in a more powerful presence and more engagement. Don't be shy with the likes!

Step 3: Comment and "shoutout" regularly

There is also an option to "comment" on posts - it's the icon shaped like a word bubble. In your comments you can hashtag, as well.

Don't be surprised if at first you don't get many comments. Instagram is actually a reasonably quick platform when it comes to generating "likes" - you'll get "likes" faster on Instagram as compared to Facebook, for instance. However, actual commenting tends to be a bit slower just because it's more effort.

However, once you do start getting comments, you'll want to comment back. This will encourage your followers to interact with you, since you will specifically be paying attention to them. It's a personal touch.

You should also do "shoutouts" to people on Instagram. You can accomplish this by using the "@" symbol. So if somebody wanted to give Bob at Bob's Widgets a "shoutout," they would use

"@bobswidgetsboston" to get his attention.

In the event that Instagrammers participated in Bob's Widget Bonanza and hashtagged their photos with #bobswidgetbonanza, then Bob should absolutely repost their photos in his own Instagram feed and credit the original poster with the "@" symbol. People are thrilled when brands repost their content.

Step 4: Don't get banned

You definitely want to ensure that you are playing by the rules of the Instagram platform or you risk getting banned. Sometimes this simply means that your account will be disabled for a few hours, and other times it can be for weeks. Here are some tips to avoid the dreaded block or ban:

1.Don't start interacting with other profiles right away. Instead, spend some time building up your own feed. "Fake" profiles tend to neglect their own feeds and start harassing users.

2.Complete your Instagram profile. Spam profiles tend to have empty feeds and empty profile bios.

3.Do not post multiple duplicate comments. While it's okay to tell somebody "nice photo," do not tell 30 people in one sitting "nice photo." This will get the attention of the bots.

4.Follow the community guidelines for Instagram. These are clearly posted on the website and should be followed to the letter.

Chapter 10: Ways To Lose Instagram Followers

Here we'll take a look at the top five things which can lose you Instagram followers. I know it happens, because I've personally lost followers myself when I did exactly what I'm about to explain to you.

Personal Standpoints - These can be one of the fastest ways you can lose followers, and you should never post anything which is political, religious, or anything which people will side on, argumentatively speaking. It can be something as simple as "what is the best basketball team?" But because people have opinions, and they don't like being placed in a situation where they have to choose, it is far better to remain neutral (as much as possible). In this way, no one needs to take sides or take offense and unfollow you because of it.

Posting Multiple Pictures - You should only aim to post pictures every few hours because followers become annoyed when the same person posts picture after picture. It seems strange when Instagram is all about displaying images, but that's the way it is. To be safe, and to make sure you don't lose followers, post images or videos in no less than three-hour intervals.

Reply to Comments - If a person says something nice about one of your posts, you should forget just liking their comments as it doesn't look very good. Actually, because they have taken the time to write something about your post, the least you can do is make the time and reply in the same manner. Respect goes a long way and is definitely a two-way street. There is another plus (aside from being courteous), and this is that your reply makes two comments, and if you ask them a question, they will respond, which increases the number again.

Reply to a DM - When a person takes the trouble to DM (direct message) you, you should take the time to DM them back. If it seems your messages are dragging on, be sure not to reply with a question because this will encourage them to respond back, multiple times. Reply to a comment to be polite and show that the conversation (for now) is over. Just make sure to reply the first time, though.

Low-Resolution Pictures - It's been said before about picture quality, and it's such a big thing that it's worth mentioning one more time. Never post low-quality pictures, you'll lose followers because of this. And no one wants to look at pictures which make you look like a character from a 1980s video game! Or pictures that are so blurry it's painful. All images should be high in quality and not purely a picture of yourself. Make them funky and exciting, so it sparks a viewer's imagination.

To add to this, Instagram is full of pictures of models and people who are into photography, so followers are more likely to choose them over pixelated pictures, no matter who you are. And "that's just the way the cookie crumbles" at this moment in time. Remember, knowledge is power. When you have knowledge you have leverage.

9How to Boost the Number of Comments on Instagram

The number one way of increasing the numbers of comments you receive on Instagram is to comment back when somebody comments on one of your pictures. This gives double the number of comments in your feed, and not everyone looks at it that way. If someone goes back to your image and looks at the total count, it will now say one hundred, as an example, whereas it would have said fifty had you not replied with a comment for each comment. This gives the impression that everyone's joining into the conversation.

Number two can take a little effort and will test your memory, too. If a person likes one of your pictures, it might be the last time they like a picture or even see another one of yours for a while. If you notice a person who has liked an image that you don't recognize, you should go to their profile and like three of their pictures and leave three comments. When you do this, the law of reciprocity comes into play again, and they will be more inclined to visit and comment on another one of your images. Hopefully!!

When you make a post, you should enter something which makes use of a blank space. A good example being: "My Favorite type of pizza is …" There are many people who will respond to this comment because they want to answer the question you have asked. This will ultimately increase your number of comments. Food might not be the best example, and if you are in a specific niche, it could be something which is related to this that starts up a conversation.

When you make a post, the first comments you make are supposed to be your hashtags, and you're not supposed to include them in your caption, as we went over (a little earlier on). The next tip adds on from this. And it's regarding the four comments following your hashtags... these should be lines of colorful emojis. What this does is create four different comments which cover your hashtags, so no one can see which you have used, and also because: as a person is scrolling through their feed, the different colors catch their attention. This makes them pause by your picture which might lead to a comment being posted from them. I know this technique works because I use it on each and every picture I've posted ;)

The next tip has also been mentioned, and it involves a call to action. When you use these, it makes the person who is reading your post want to perform the action you state. This could merely be to post a comment (or something similar) at the end of every caption. This works, and it does work well because it's also a significant thing on YouTube, and it reminds a person to perform the action before they click to another page.

The next tip is the use of a funny picture. If you post this, ask people to caption it, and the top three will get a shoutout. These top three you put inside your caption and then they have the chance to grow their followers too. Everyone wins! Additionally, it also adds and inspires extra conversations to your post and adds likes to your post, as well.

Next, is a reminder about creating a group with twenty or thirty like-minded people, and when you post, you'll then need to DM them all to like your picture and to leave comments. If you all do it together, it's a great way of increasing comments. As a side note, Instagram's algorithm notices this page action and gives you the chance to be seen by more people, too. While we are on this topic, there is no saying you only have to create one group, you can create as many as you think you can cope with. "The world is your oyster," metaphorically speaking!

Next is a follow-on from the first tip. When you respond to a person's comment, you should ask them a question, and this will encourage them to answer. Here you are increasing your comments each time. One tip here is to ask a question regarding something else which will draw others into the conversation and create a thread, and this is where you can increase your comments five-fold for each picture that you post.

Another great tip; is about using all the available characters you can within your caption. You can add something inspirational or thought-provoking which gives the viewer another reason to leave a comment. Now they have two reasons, rather than just one. Make the caption as good as you can, and they might get some benefit from what you have to say.

Lastly, tag as many people as you can in the picture. This notifies them you have posted something, and that you want them to check out the picture and leave a comment for you. It's also a great way of informing everyone in your group, automatically, without direct messaging each one separately.

Chapter 11: Influencers

When it comes to Instagram marketing, one of the biggest markets is the influencer market. Making sure that you use Instagram influencers for marketing your product or for growing your page can help you tremendously when it comes to building your brand or making you more recognized. That being said, there are specific ground rules to look at when it comes to finding the right Instagram marketing for your needs. So in this chapter, we will talk about what to look out for when hiring Instagram influencers and how to get the best return from it. With that being said, let us talk about how to find the right influencer for your niche and how to go about advertising with them.

How to Find the Right Influencer?

One of the things to look out for when looking for influencers is if they have a following. Not many people realize this, but having a massive following does not equal a good return. For instance, as you know, many people can buy Instagram followers who are not engaged and will not react to any post, which is why when you look out for Instagram influencers, do you look for accounts that have a big following and get a ton of engagement? You can check the engagement by going online and looking at the engagement calculator. There are many calculators online that will tell you what the engagement rate is for a specific account. If you are looking to get a good deal and a good return on your investment, then make sure that you look for accounts that have at least a 2 % engagement rate. The 2 % engagement rate is for accounts that have at least fifty thousand followers to a million followers.

Once you have checked if the account has the right number of following, and the engagement rate is reasonable, then you can proceed with the negotiation and figuring out the right price for your shoutout. Keep in mind that the average rate for a shoutout is around $40 with a story swipe up. If an account below a million is asking for more than $40 for a story shoutout, chances are, they do not know what they are talking about, and you should look for other accounts. This is true for most of the niches; however, if you are in the makeup niche, then the prices will be a little bit higher.

To find out the right price for your niche, asked many influencers what their rates are, and they will give you the cost. Once you've got the price, average out all the influencers' rates and go from there. Make sure that when you are looking for influencers, you are looking for influencers in your niche. One of the worst things you can do is for you to start looking for influencers who are not in your niche. The truth is they will gladly take your money, but you will not get any return from it.

Overall, make sure that you are looking for people who are in your niche.

Finally, the last thing to remember when looking for Instagram influencers is how open they are with you. If they are in it to grab your money and are not willing to negotiate the price, then there is a chance that they will not be the type of person you will want to work with. Most of the time, influencers will level with you and come out with a better price, which is why it is so crucial that you negotiate when looking for influencers and getting the best bang for your buck. If you are not negotiating the price, then you are leaving money on the table. Let us avoid that. These are the basic rules for finding the right influencers. Make sure that you use all the advice provided to you in this section, as it will help you to save a lot of money but, more specifically, get a better return on your investment.

Why Should You Use Influencers?

Many people might be wondering why is it so crucial for them to hire an influencer and promote their product or their page. The truth is that Instagram influencers can be a fantastic tool when it comes to growing your page or your business. The great thing about Instagram influencers is that they have a broad engaged audience that will be ready to buy your products or start following you. This is something you can't rule out in regards to growing your business. Make sure that you use Instagram influencers, especially in the beginning, as they are very crucial for your growth. More often than not, you will not have an idea of how to market your page using Instagram ads. Granted, we have given you the tools for it, but that does not mean that you will be successful from the get-go. What Instagram influencers can do is give you the warm traffic that is ready to follow you or buy from you. Once you have gotten enough sales or enough followers, you will have a better chance of being successful with Instagram ads. The more deals you have in your pixel, the better the chances of being successful in your Instagram ads. Influencer marketing can facilitate that for you.

Moreover, in the beginning, you will have a better return on investment if you use Instagram influencers. Instagram influencers are straightforward to use and can be very reliable, which is why you should not ignore this and utilize it in the beginning, and even when you are more successful. To this day, many businesses like Nike use Instagram influencers to grow their page and business, so do not rule out the possibility of Instagram influencers. The reason that they work is that they have a warm audience ready to buy, an audience that trusts their word. Also, they have spent years and years growing their page, so they know what they are talking about.

Shoutout for a Shoutout

If you are not aware of this method, then let me clarify it for you. This method requires you to give a person shoutout, and in return, they give you a shoutout. This is a great way to grow your page or to get more sales without spending a lot of money. This method has been used by many people to get a ton of deals on their page and to grow their page without spending a lot of money. If you do not have a lot of money to start with, then this method can work significantly for you when it comes to influencer marketing. The great thing about influencer marketing is that you do not need a lot of capital to get started. You can have no money and still see great results, which is why you must use Instagram marketing to work toward your advantage. In this instance, you can see that having no money makes no difference when it comes to Instagram influencer marketing, as he or she can do something called a shoutout for a shoutout. However, there are specific rules to this method, so let us talk about it. The first thing you need to make sure when doing a shoutout for a shoutout is that you both need to have a similar following.

Do not expect a page with a million followers to give you a shoutout when you only have a thousand followers. If you only have a thousand followers, then make sure that you partner up with someone who has two thousand followers or at least close to it. Now, if you are wondering how the returns will come from someone who only has a thousand followers, then let me tell you that it will be pretty good. This method, although it will not work as well as someone who has a million followers, will slowly yield you a good return, and you are a free investment.

You will indeed get some followers and some sales. This is for people who do not have any money and yet want to grow their Instagram page. If you are in that bucket, then make sure they use this method by messaging a lot of people, with the same following, to give you a shoutout. One thing you need to make sure is that the person you were going to do a shoutout for does not have any fake followers. The best way to check that out is to ask them their "top countries by follows." If most of them are from India or China, then chances are, they have bought the followers. You do not want someone who has a lot of bot followers.

Chapter 12: More Tips For Utilizing Instagram

Comment Everywhere

Comments are the main thing that gets you noticed under hashtags. Not just other people commenting on your stuff, but you commenting on other people's stuff. This is where you have to be able to handle talking to other people, even if they are strangers. Which tends to be easier if you are behind a screen because you are literally talking to your keyboard and the internet communicates for you. However, mean comments still hurt, so you have to be sure to put on your thick skin before going out there and commenting on things.

Comments are important because people you would not come across normally are now exposed to your page, and you can get some more publicity, and more followers this way. You want to get people from all walks of life, and if you do not comment on random things, then you will end up with only a certain group of people, and you want to be inclusive. So comments are essential to not only gaining followers but as a direct result, they are essential for business.

Just like with any of these tips, there are some things that you should keep in mind before you just dive in headfirst. If you keep these things in mind, you should have no problem getting noticed with your comments.

☐ Variety is key: You have to add some variety on the types of profiles that you comment on. Even if they do not really interest you, you want to interact with the people interacting with that page. You want to get your business info out as far and wide as it will spread, so branch out from your own hobbies and favorite celebrities, and choose some different ones that have a lot of followers and commenters and begin commenting as well to get noticed. You just have to know something basic about what you are commenting on to get people's attention, and if you don't maybe try to make a pun from what was posted. That helps as well. When in doubt, joke it out (or trend it out if you prefer).

☐   Avoid Spamming: Spam is when someone comments on one post the same thing over and over again. This is considerably annoying. No one wants to follower someone who spams their page, nor do they want that person following them. There are certain etiquette rules that you need to follow when commenting on someone's post, and if you do not follow them, not only could you lose followers, you could get your profile shut down. You do not want that because often times you have to create a new one to get back up and running on Instagram.

So how do you avoid this? It is simple, just don't spam. This tip is all about how to avoid becoming a spammer, and how to keep people from ignoring and blocking you.

First off, always make sure that what you are commenting is related to the post, and not something that is entirely unrelated. This is important because if you comment, "check out my gear" on a post about puppies, people are going to assume that you are a bot or a spammer, and they will completely ignore your post. Even if it is just mentioning something that was said in the post and tying it back to what you want to say is better than just putting a random comment. You have to make what you are saying relevant. Think of it as having a regular conversation. You don't want to be talking about real estate, and then have someone come up and say "dude I just bought this delicious candy bar." You would look at that person like they were crazy, and you would probably not even acknowledge that they said anything at all. Same thing with comments. You have to keep with the flow of conversation.

You should also never comment more than once on any given post until you are addressed by someone in the comments. You should always make sure that you are not over commenting as well, and having a conversation with someone on a public feed. This is considered spam and could irritate the original poster. While everyone wants comments, they don't want to have to scroll through comments that have nothing to do with what they posted, or a million links on their post to get to what other people have to say. They want to be able to see what all was said without having to scroll for hours, so make sure that you only comment once, and don't carry on a conversation in the comments.

Don't comment on everything that someone posts. This can make them uncomfortable, especially if they do not know you at all, and are not following you. It will put on what is known as "stalker status" which basically means that you are acting like a stalker and freaking them out. This can lead them to leave a bad review of your page on their profile after they block you, which is not a good thing, and if you have mutual followers, it could cause you to lose those followers, as they too will feel creeped out by your blatant disregard for comment etiquette.

Be careful when you are commenting that your comments make you seem like a genuine person trying to interact, and not like a page that is run by a robot. You have to give people the human element to attract followers, otherwise, it is all for naught, and you will not be able to sell as much as you had hoped.

☐   Use Famous Profiles: These can be profiles of big businesses, famous people, Instafamous people, anything that you choose, as long as the profile has over a hundred thousand followers. These will be the gold mines in the comment sections. There will be so many people that will visit the comment section on these pages that you can't help but get noticed. This will help boost your views and follows to a higher amount than if you commented on the page of someone who only has a hundred followers. If you comment on like, say, Miley Cyrus's profile, then you will have millions of people viewing your comment an hour. This means that you are bound to get some new followers. The more you comment on famous profiles, the better your chances of getting noticed by other people.

If you comment on famous people's profile be sure to do so without becoming a spammer. It is so easy to get caught up in the feeling that you are getting swept away in the current of comments, but believe me, if you keep posting it will be even worse. People will see your comment, don't worry.

☐ Comment First: Okay, so you don't necessarily have to get the first comment every time, you just should try your best to be in the top fifteen comments most of the time. This is called the elite comment section. It gets the most views out of any other comments, and more views mean more followers. Let's put this into perspective. If you regularly comment on a hundred photos, you may be able to get ten followers for every hundred you comment on. However, if you comment in the elite section of one photo that will be heavily trafficked, you could get ten followers with that one comment. So instead of a one is to ten ratio, it then becomes a ten is to one ratio. The odds are way better with the second one.

These are the keys to commenting successfully on Instagram posts. If you follow these tips, then you should have no problem whatsoever with gaining followers from your comments. You just have to time it right, use the right people, and don't be a spammer. These are the most important things to remember.

Research

It is important to do your research when you are on Instagram. This will help you in your endeavors to gather a larger following to promote your business more than you already do. You have to visit other profiles with high followings and see how they make their success. It involves a bit of spy work because not many people like to share their secrets, because then they would not be secrets anymore. This tip is here to show you how to go about researching other profiles to find the best way for you to gather more followers on your page.

Shadow the Big Stores

There is no escaping the fact that you are going to end up following a few big box stores on your Instagram, so why not use it to your advantage? There are so many big stores out there, and most of the time they don't even pay attention to who is following them, so there is no harm in following them to shadow their technique. They are giant stores, generally with a huge following, so what is the harm in you following them to figure out how you can make your fan base a little bigger? Nothing. There is no harm in doing so. In fact, you can gain a lot from this, and you should feel smart, not embarrassed to be following a chain of stores to note their techniques.

First, make a note of the human element in the profile. Some profiles are completely automated; some are actually run by a response team made up of actual humans. You should find that the one made up of actual humans has a bigger following, and not only that, it probably has more interactions. If you want a bigger following with better interactions, stay away from automation. This is one of the most important things that you can do. Keep the human element in your profile.

Secondly, note how they post. Is it always something that is related to their store, or does they post other things as well? Note how that affects following rates from other stores that only post their goods. You should find that the more interactive profiles have a larger following as well, which would go to show you that you don't always have to post about your product. Post about what is going on in the world as well. You will find your followers are a little more interactive then.

Pay attention to how they respond to questions. Do they reply with the same link no matter what the question is, or do they try to answer it the best they can right there in the comments to save their customers time and frustration? The second option tends to have a better satisfaction rate than the first. You have to make sure that you are following this as well. As easy as it would be to direct them to a self-help page that you have set up, people prefer the one on one connection from getting a real response from someone. This will significantly help your following if you choose to do this. I mean, it is your brand, shouldn't you know everything there is to know about it especially if you created it? Give people some of your time, and you will have some repeat customers.

Check out the Competition

This is another thing you should do if there are people selling a similar product to what you are selling. By doing this, you can see where you are ahead, and where you are behind. This will tell you what you need to fix and help you decide what you need to do to gain more followers. This is important because you want your page to be the best because you want people to want to choose your product, not the competitors.

Check out to see who they are following, and try to follow those same people. Comment on the same things that they are commenting on, and get people to choose you over the competition. Be careful though; you don't want to step over any copyright infringement lines, so always be cautious.

So that is how you market on Instagram. Remember that marketing on Instagram can get you a lot of business if you do it right. So always remember to be real, be active, and be interactive. Do not automate your profile, and do not ignore the people who follow you, as they are your business. You have to stay humble.

Chapter 13: Best Practices For Using Instagram

Social media has proven to be a fast and efficient marketing tool for businesses of any size. For individuals, it is a savvy means to stay in touch with the people you know. Instagram is one of the more popular new kids on the block as far as social media is concerned. One of the reasons that Instagram is so popular is that it uses photos to convey a message. This is a marketer's dream as photos and pictures tend to attract more attention and draw more people as compared to textual content.

As a person, you may also benefit from growing your profile by using Instagram. Using Instagram on Facebook will increase the visibility of your profile since people share and interact with photos more than any other content that is available. The app allows you to run your photos through a filter, which in essence, just edits them so they look better and more professional. You can also share photos on your Twitter account so that you can garner more interest and get more people to follow you.

Everything is more visually focused

As a small business, social media is one of the most effective marketing tools that you can use without spending too much. Instagram allows you to keep your clients updated on what is new. You can upload many photos in a day to keep people interested in what is new with your business and for any new developments. However, ensure that you do not share too many photos so that you give people enough time to see them and respond to them. It is important to be consistent so that your clients also know what to expect in terms of posting photos, new information, or any other news.

You can also share some photos of the behind the scenes of your business so that your clients and customers feel much more like a part of your business, which will make them more likely to become loyal customers. You can also show them how to use a product, photos of an event that you are having or something else that is not public information and is more personal, such as photos of your office or employees. This shows people the human side of your business which would make them want to keep checking back, or they want to follow your profile to see what new things they can learn or discover. "As a personal brand, give them insights into how you think, decide and discern"

Instagram is also a great way to share some of the work you have done. This, in essence, shows others what you can do and will sell your work to potential clients. Engage your followers to promote brand loyalty; for example, responding to a comment made on your product. This also works for a personal profile; to get people to follow you and interact with your

Instagram profile. Of course, you also have to interact with them, follow them, and comment on their photos.

Since your Instagram profile can only be viewed by the people you are friends within your fans and followers list, it is best used with another type of social media such as Facebook since so many more people will be able to see and respond to your photos.

First point of contact

You can use Instagram to direct people to your personal blog, other social media such as Pinterest, or your company website. In both of these cases, the photos act as a bait to get people interested in you so that you can then introduce other content. You can also use hashtags to trend a photo or connect different photos that are related in some way which you would like people to see. It also attracts like-minded people as they will gravitate to hashtags on things they are interested in.

It is best to take good, clear photos on Instagram. A badly taken photograph cannot be salvaged by the filter function in Instagram. People will respond more to photos that are well taken. You also need to keep abreast on what is relevant and interesting to your followers so ask for feedback and understand what they are saying so that you can post photos that keep them interested in your profile. You can also make your photos fun by experimenting with creative photo shots.

HOW TO GET INSTAGRAM FOLLOWERS?

If you want to reach out a wider audience, you have to start collecting your Instagram followers.

Here are a few legit and tried and tested techniques to get Instagram followers fast.

1. Public accounts. First of all If you have a private account, only your friends wil see what you share. Hence, the first step to getting Instagram followers fast is to go public. For those of your really worried about privacy, you can always keep a check on what you choose to share.

2. Hashtags. Instagram uses hashtags to filter photographs. When you search for photographs, the social media network will display all the photographs with a common hashtag. Popularity is not the only criteria when selecting the hashtags to go with your photographs. You should also use relevant ones. 3 is an ideal number of hashtags to use with your photograph.

3. Regular uploads. A dormant account doesn't usually get too many followers. Instagrammers on a regular basis tend to unfollow inactive accounts. Hence, the strategy is to refresh your account with new, original and captivating content.

As a rule of the thumb, don't post too little and don't flood your page. A photo daily is a good standard.

4. Use filters. Why you should use filters? Well, they really improve the look of your photos adding a more personalized touch. This sense of added beauty is enough to draw more followers who love following quality work. Check how a particular filter looks before you actually apply it.

5. Picture collages. Instead of uploading alone picture, you can combine multiple images into a single one. Such images are more engaging as they tell a story. There are several paid and free, third-party collage makers and photo-editing apps you can use for the purpose.

6. Time it right. The most breathtaking photographs will have no viewers if you post it when the entire Instagram community is asleep. The peak times on Instagram are in the morning before work and in the evening after work. This is when most Instagrammers check their accounts. So, time your uploads right.

7. Follow, like and comment. Yet another tip to increase your visibility on Instagram is to follow others. They might follow you in return. Take it a step further by liking and commenting on other's photos and videos. You're likely to grab the attention of the photo owner as well his/her followers. It might prompt them to check out your Instagram account, increasing the likelihood of followers.

8. Sync with Facebook. With Facebook taking over Instagram, you can now share your photographs across both the platforms by integrating your Facebook and Instagram account. This way your Instagram activity gets streamed on to Facebook. Facebook Friends that also have an Instagram account will start following you, if they like what you upload.

9. Call to Action. Your captions should have a strong Call To action. You should aim for better engagement with your captions. In that, they should compel them to comment or start an interesting discussion.

So, these are different ways in which you can get Instagram followers fast. You can also join micro-blogging groups and participate in discussions there.

Instagram, the photo-sharing site had gained immense popularity over the last few years. With most social networking sites, the more followers you have, the more you are able to leverage their potential.

SEO TIPS FOR USING INSTAGRAM

Search engine optimization is simply a process of making your blog more visible to search engines for particular targeted keywords or phrases. In other words, SEO is just a popularity contest among websites. The question is always which website is the most popular and relevant for specific keywords or phrases, according to a particular search engine? If the question is placed in this way and not in terms of SEO strategies and techniques, you will realize that SEO goes beyond quality content and link building.

It is not surprising that with the growth of social media networks, many people are utilizing these social media websites to reinforce their SEO efforts. The good news is that you do not need SEO training to make use of these social media websites because it takes very little to get the hang of these sites.

Although some big companies hire an SEO company to manage their social media pages, there is no reason why you cannot do it to increase the popularity of your own website.

One particular social media site that has grown in popularity since it made its debut in 2010 is Instagram, a photo sharing social media website. Instagram started out as a mobile application for Apple users but then support was added in 2012 so that Android users can use it as well. Although the effect of Instagram on actual search engine rankings is debatable, it is a great tool for promoting your website, products, services, and basically, increasing your website's popularity and generating organic traffic. Below are some tips to help you use Instagram in promoting your website.

1. Create a focused theme. If your Instagram account is for your website or business then make it evident from the get-go. Make sure that another Instagram user visiting your profile page will have no doubt in his or her mind what your account is all about. This means limiting your non-website related posts.

2. Describe your images. Since Instagram is a photo sharing service, the only way to put content is to accurately describe your images or photos. Never post a picture that has no description. Even a single-word description is much better than none.

3. Make proper use of hashtags. Hashtags are popularly used to associate your image to a particular topic or subject. You can think of these hashtags as keywords in the usual way you would promote your website.

4. Engage with other users. Go beyond just posting images. Connect with other users by commenting on images of others and by responding to comments on your images.

HOW TO INCREASE INSTAGRAM FOLLOWERS WITHOUT SPENDING MONEY

Instagram has over eight hundred million active users. The stats on Instagram could be described as highly impressive and encouraging. A little break down will surprise you and at the same time get you excited. Instagram has over 500 million active users with over 300 million active users daily, 80% of those users are outside the USA, 4.2 billion likes everyday and over 95 million photos and videos uploaded every day. This is simply wonderful and a goldmine for online marketers and business.

Those statistics should send a signal to your nerves and let you understand how important Instagram could be for your business.

The issue is that, how do you get on Instagram and acquire followers that will become your loyal customers. I will be showing you how to do that in the following steps and guidelines

1. Signup with Facebook: This is the most easiest and quickest way to set up your Instagram account. It will automatically allow you to follow your friends that are already on Instagram and in turn they will follow you too. Your friends and family will be the first followers on Instagram which will help boost your profile and get you ready for the main deal

2. Quality Photos: the most important thing on Instagram is the quality of your photos, make sure your photos are of high quality before posting them on Instagram. Having quality photos on Instagram help you get more likes, comments and more followers which will help push you up the ladder and on top of all your competitors within the same niche. If you are taking the pictures with a camera, make sure the lighting and focus are right to get you the right photos you need to go viral on Instagram.

3. Like other Photos: I call this trick notice me. Is like your first day in school, no one knows you and the only way people will start interacting with you is by you taking the first step to say hi or introduce yourself to them.

When you like other people photos, those people visit your profile and decide to follow and also like your photos. This is how you start growing your network on Instagram

4. Follow Others: This is the fastest ways to increase your followers on Instagram. When you follow others, they decide to follow you back and create a connection between you both. This helps increase your followers and likes on photos you have on your profile. Follow others to get more followers

5. Comment on other Photos: This method takes more time and work but it surely pays off. When you comment on other people's photos, you increase the chance of them following you and liking your photos too. Just take some time out of your social media marketing timetable and comment on other people photos to increase your followers

6. Use relevant Hashtags: Hashtags have come a long way on social media and Instagram is not an exception. Making use of relevant hashtags help get you more visibility and popular on Instagram. The more hashtags you use, the more popular your photos will become. This means more likes, more followers and more comments which all help boost your profile

7. Exchange Shoutouts: This is simply a method to promote others while they promote you too. It's simply a win-win situation for both members. This method helps in promoting your profile. You need to find people within your niche and reach out to them and ask for a shoutout. You can simply do this by sending them an email or request on Instagram.

HOW TO MAKE YOUR BRAND BIGGER AND TO DRIVE SALES USING INSTAGRAM

We are talking about brand awareness through social media. It is, in my opinion, the coolest way to reach a maximum number of people in the meantime. There is a lot of struggle in the market to make your brand bigger than others and keep the folks stick to your content. Instagram is the freshest and trending platform in the world of social media to reach the people worldwide with the crisp stuff you want to serve. After all, who would not love to see his products seen by more people? Nevertheless, handling the competition successfully is not everyone's cup of tea.

HOT TIPS TO MARKET YOUR BRAND PERFECTLY ON INSTAGRAM:

1. Complete your bio profile: Sharing ample information about you in your bio will leave a hint for the people about what you do and what you serve. Choose the Instagram name of your account carefully so followers can recognize you easily. You can opt for the product name or any name related to your business that is common across all other social media channels. Do not forget to share the link of your website or homepage in the bio to get traffic directly.

2. Show your potential: Every business has a story to tell or moments to share to spread inspiration or information to the world. Use your Instagram account for such purposes and let the followers see your first step to the success. This shows you ingenuity and proves you are not only a bunch of robots pushing your product or service. This trick also helps to built stronger relations with the customers and of course a seal of trust.

3. Grow your followers like crazy: Unlike Facebook, Instagram feed changes faster and you are buried soon. Use hashtags to increase the freshness and shelf life of your posts. This widens your discoverability with the communities linked by such keywords. You are more likely to be visible for slightly longer. However, using more than one hashtag is not a good idea and overusing the tool goes down on posts.

BRINGS YOUR BRAND TO LIFE USING INSTAGRAM

It seems that each year there is a new social media "star." Facebook, Twitter, and LinkedIn rose to stardom in recent years, and 2012 the year of Pinterest. Now, Instagram is gunning for top billing.

What opportunities does this present to marketers? With the Instagram community thriving, major brands and companies like Starbuck, MTV, Nike and Marc Jacobs, to name just a few, are jumping on board aggressively adopting the mobile photo app into their marketing strategies.

According to Simply Measured, 59% of the Top 100 Global Interbrand Brands already have Instagram accounts. And based on the Instagram blog, the two-plus-year-old platform reaches over 100 million active users each month. Compare that to Twitter, which broke the 200 million mark after six years.

What makes Instagram different from other social media networks? Most obvious is that it's almost entirely photo-based. But beyond of that, its simplicity makes it an effective vehicle for engaging consumers since they can express themselves from anywhere, anytime.

WHY SHOULD YOUR BUSINESS USE INSTAGRAM?

Visual content is expected to be a major trend in 2018 and beyond. Pictures appeal to emotions and resonate across cultures. In fact, if we take a look at social networks overall, photos drive more engagement than any other form of content. On Facebook, for example, photos have an interaction rate 39% higher than other posts. It is not surprising, then, to see Instagram rise to popularity so quickly.

If you're looking for inspiration about how to grow your current Instagram community check out examples from four brands that are successfully integrating the platform into their marketing mix:

1. Red Bull. Through a recent Instagram contest, Red Bull gave away two tickets to this year's Red Bull King of the Rock Finals basketball tournament in San Francisco. Followers were asked to take a picture of themselves with a basketball in unexpected locations and tag their photos #TakeMeToTheRock. The contest not only got followers excited, it also let Red Bull make a statement to and connect with the sports community.

2. Ford Fiesta. In early 2012, Fiestagram was one of the first Instagram campaigns executed by a big brand. Ford engaged its target audience with a simple photo competition. Approximately 16,000 photos were posted during the seven-week campaign and the promotion received great visibility on Facebook and Twitter as well, with many users linking their social networks.

3. Tiffany & Co. A Tiffany campaign offered followers 3 new photo filters: Tiffany blue, peach, and black and white. Followers were encouraged to tag photos of themselves and their significant others (#TrueLovePictures) and Tiffany featured a selection on its "True Love in Pictures" website. The effort enabled Tiffany to give its followers relevant, brand-related content, while also inviting them to take part in the experience.

4. Comodo. The Soho, NY eatery recently created an "Instagram menu" by asking clients to snap photos of their meals and tag them with the hashtag #comodomenu. Now, diners and curious prospective customers at this Latin American restaurant can enjoy a more interactive dining experience by searching the hashtag to see photos of the restaurant's offerings.

MUST-USE INSTAGRAM TOOLS

Instagram has become a very popular photo sharing platform today with more than 500 million users and 16 million images shared. It has not only attracted individual users but as well as business organizations, business owners and has in fact made marketers rethink their strategies.

According to Google Trends, the volume of searches for Instagram has grown tremendously and this trend is expected to continue this year. Sharing photos on Instagram may be enough for some of you but there are tools you can still use to attract more people to your brand and convert them to clients or customers.

1. Statigr.am

This web-based management tool offers much functionality that enables users to better interact with various content on the Instagram platform.

It has a Viewer that lets you see your feed and the people connected to you, add or remove new followers or do other actions on images/videos such as liking, sharing, commenting or reposting them.

The Statistics section lets you view stats on the most popular content, how engaging your content is and the number of your followers.

The Promote functionality allows Instagram users to promote their account even to people who are non-users of the platform. It lets non-Instagram user's view and comment on photos on Facebook. Additionally, it allows the installation of an app on Facebook from Statig.ram to display photos on a separate tab or create a photo gallery that can be included in a blog or website.

The Manage feature, meanwhile, lets users interact with the most recent comments on various posts on the platform.

2. Repost

Repost is a mobile application ideal for Android and iOS devices. It lets users repost content from their community as well as like and comment on photos.

The advantage of this tool is it gives the full attribution to the person who posted the image.

In fact, this part can be customized such as where to put the attribution and whether to darken or lighten the background for such attribution.

3. Postso

If you think that scheduling posts is only possible on Facebook or via a third party app, you can actually do so on Instagram through the Postso tool.

Most Instagram users have the habit of posting their newly taken photos on the platform right away. But you can always share your other photos at a later time and you can do this through Postso.

To use it, simply connect your Instagram account with Postso after logging in. You can even connect it to your Twitter and Facebook account.

After uploading and providing captions to your images and adding a location if you want, you can then specify a time you want certain photos to display on your Instagram account. The time is at 30-minute intervals.

4. Iconosquare

This is a very popular web interface for Instagram with several useful features. It showcases an individual photo viewer that lets you like, comment and share photos on different social networking sites.

Iconosquare also has a statistics tab that displays a user's activity and information on each activity in the last seven days. In addition, it provides monthly stats on the number of photos posted, the engagement on those images and density of when you post together with tag, filter, and geolocation usage.

Chapter 14: Rules You Should Know While Posting On Instagram

Instagram has provided some new examples of creative ways to use Instagram Stories ads. Nowadays it is one of the best methods for generating traffic on your blogs or websites.

1. Don't use banned hashtags on the post

Not all hashtags are created equal. Using one of Instagram's banned hashtags can land you in hot water and ignorance is not an excuse.

While some banned hashtags are pretty common sense and align with Instagram's terms of service, others aren't so obvious. According to the HuffPo, the banned list includes #adulting, #citycentre, and #eggplant. Research the hashtags you use carefully, make sure that they are relevant to your audience and don't have a secret, urban dictionary or emoji meaning you didn't know about...

2. Use a third party posting app

Instagram has a closed API- it doesn't allow third-party apps to post directly to Instagram. You can still use a social media dashboard like Agorapulse to manage your Instagram account but the process is a little bit more complicated than for Facebook or Twitter. Most legit social media management apps work around the challenge. For example, you can log into your Agorapulse account and schedule an Instagram post.

When the time comes, you'll receive a notification. You can then log into the Agorapulse app which will take you to Instagram where you can hit publish. The key is that you have to be the one that hits publish.

But, while that's how we do it, there are some apps like Schedugram that post directly to Instagram for you, using your username and password to access your account. This is a big Terms and Conditions no. Jumping through a few extra hoops can be frustrating but it keeps your account safe.

3. Don't post too much content

Instagram favors real, human posters and all the dos and don'ts are meant to prioritize them over spammers and bots. Whereas Twitter has apps like Social Quant that can automatically follow and unfollow a bunch of people to build up your following, Instagram frowns on that kind of behavior. That's why they have an unofficial cap on account activity.

What exactly are those numbers? While Instagram hasn't released official numbers Ana Gotter did some in-depth research and came up with the following:

Following and unfollowing over 60 people an hour

Liking more than 300 posts an hour

Posting over 60 comments an hour

4. Stay away from the robots

Look. In any other circumstances, I'll be the first to point out the potential of bots in automating your marketing process but that's not what Instagram is all about.

INSTAGRAM TIPS FOR AN ONLINE BUSINESS

I want to talk about a fast-growing social media site that is really growing fast and offers really good online promotion potential for any business. I'm talking about Instagram!

Before we get to that when it comes to marketing a business online many of the old paid to advertise online still work. Pay per click ads on Google, and Yahoo/Bing still work. PPC ads on Facebook really work.

However, there is no denying the power of Facebook, Twitter, YouTube, LinkedIn, Pinterest, and so on. The same is true for Instagram. Instagram has come to stay and has over 500 million users worldwide.

Meaning, displaying your business products and services online through Instagram photos has a wide reach all over the world.

Here are some important Instagram tips for an online business.

1. Share your photos on other social networks. Ideally, you want your business to be popular among many people, including those that are not on Instagram.

To achieve this, share the important information regarding your products and services on other social networks such as Twitter and Facebook. Doing this allows people who are not Instagram subscribers to see your photos and click on your link, which may lead to improved sales and profit.

2. Use hashtags. Use specific hashtags as they will help you get more followers on Instagram to share your photos with.

When using hashtags be sure to avoid general statements such as #television, instead say #Samsung #LCD. Try as much as possible to engage your followers by using effective hashtags. Also, be sure to check what other firms in your industry are doing. They might have new ideas that you don't know.

3. Only Share important content. Intuitively, many people will only want to know the most important information about your business, goods, and service.

When sharing information on Instagram be sure you only share important information regarding the business, its goods, and service. Avoid using sharing of information that cannot add value to the business.

4. Be consistent. Consistency is very important when it comes to increasing sales and business popularity through any social network.

Be sure the photos you post and share on Instagram tell the same story about your business. Posting inconsistent and incoherent information can be costly, so always make sure you stick to the same information you want to tell people regarding your business.

Follow these Instagram tips for an online business to get in the photo-sharing social media game. They work!

DOES INSTAGRAM WORK FOR NETWORK MARKETING COMPANIES?

Does Instagram work for network marketing companies? Great question! Some people are very serious about building their business offline but are not sure if this social media platform will be helpful.

Instagram is a very powerful tool to use to grow your network marketing company. People think in pictures and when you have social media at your fingertips you will be able to use this platform to get more people to pay attention to you.

Promote your product

If you have visual products, you can use product pictures to promote and showcase your products and their benefits. You may even want to post some photos of yourself using the products and videos are great as well.

INSTAGRAM AS A SHOPPING PLATFORM

From being a media-sharing app for selfies and anything visually appealing, Instagram is branching out into the eCommerce field. It will soon roll out a shopping feature which online retailers and shoppers will find very convenient.

The social giant is pretty much aware that mobile commerce is going to overtake PCs in two years' time or even earlier, hence it wants to be one of its cornerstones.

What's nice about Instagram's new feature is that it could serve as a promotion channel for your products, and even more so for your online store.

As for your potential customers, they will be able to see and explore your products without having to leave Instagram for another site.

How to sell on Instagram?

The regular Instagrammers among you will find Instagram's shopping feature super easy to use. Now, if you're not a fan of this visual media sharing app, but looking into it as a potential revenue source, you just need to prepare high-quality photos which highlight your products.

To get started, upload a photo which features up to five products that you're selling. When a user clicks on the tap to view products link at the bottom left of the photo, a tag will appear on each of the items, showing the product's name and price.

Once they click on a tag, they will be taken across to a page that shows the complete description, special features and accessories-if there is any of a product.

While the customer is there, they may opt to click on the Shop Now link within the product details, which will redirect them to the product on your website where they can purchase it.

Know who buys from you

Using Instagram's shopping feature gives you the opportunity to promote your products and double your sales projection.

Aside from increasing your sales, the shopping feature also gives you access to Instagram Insights which provides crucial information that will help improve your marketing strategy.

Instagram Insights records your followers based on their demographic factors; it also shows you which of your posts draw their interest the most.

Most important of all, it lets you see who buys from your store through Instagram's shopping feature and which of your products have high demand.

Isn't that something worth exploring for your business? Are you already an

Instagrammer or planning to be one for the sake of selling more?

Brand marketing

Companies can also use Instagram pictures for their brand marketing. For example, as well as engaging an SEO agency to make sure a brand can be found in search engine results, a company could add extra appeal to their marketing with eye-catching Instagram pictures of products. These can be integrated into a social media strategy in order to encourage engagement.

Event promotion

Another way to encourage engagement using Instagram is to harness people power around upcoming events. By tying in with pre-defined and branded hashtags companies can invite users to upload their own photos of the event along with the relevant hashtag thereby igniting conversation amongst your target audiences.

User photos

188

This rapid growth, plus the fact that many people love to share photos through social media, means that you can easily find social media users who also use Instagram. Sharing cool user photos on Facebook and Twitter can be a good way for brands to engage with new people and let them know that they're appreciated. For instance, as well as running the more traditional photo competitions discussed above, you could get people to send in their favorite pictures on the understanding that you'll share the best - giving your users publicity as well as helping to promote your brand.

Behind-the-scenes info

Finally, some brands are also using Instagram to share behind-the-scenes pictures of their offices to give people more insight into what they do and help spread a more human image of their brand.

A growing number of social media agencies are using Instagram to promote their brand, and so it's definitely worth checking it out to see what the app could do for your company.

What types of business should consider using instagram and why

Instagram is one of the most misunderstood social media applications in business marketing. Some companies have just don't see the importance in investing the time and energy into selling themselves through pictures. If you are one of those companies, just remember that a picture is worth a thousand words.

What if I offer a service?

Let's take, for example, nonprofits. Nonprofit organizations work with communities and donors everyday to generate fundraising to showcase all of the great work that they do. Instagram gives nonprofit organizations the opportunity to interact with their donors and volunteers in a unique way Everyone can share the experiences that a nonprofit is working toward. If individuals are able to see nonprofit directors and employees in the field and get to know their faces personally, they are going to be far more likely to make continued contributions and wish to join the cause themselves.

Another example to use is a travel agent. Someone who is in the travel and tourism industry doesn't have a product to sell, but they have an experience that can be shared. Posting desirable photos of tropical beachside paradise destinations and showcasing customers who have used your services to visit exotic lands will entice customers to use your business. In the meantime, a travel agent can also engage on an individual level with every client or prospective client to like their travel related pictures and keep up with how their trip is going.

These are just two fields that could successfully use Instagram to their advantage. Basically any service industry or visual product could find a way to use

Instagram in their favor to increase sales and reach out to customers. Even getting the opportunity to engage customers in unique ways such as sharing promotional codes via Instagram can benefit you and your business.

Conclusion

The next step is to get online and start your own business account on Instagram. If you already have a personal account, it is best to start one that is just for business, or completely restart the personal one so that it is ready for all your business needs without mixing it with personal. Once that is done, it is time to start posting high-quality pictures to show off your products and your services, reaching out to potential customers, and bringing out your presence on this social media site.

This guidebook spent some time looking at the benefits of using Instagram marketing and why you would want to choose this for growing your business. We talked about some of the benefits of getting started with Instagram, how to start your own account, the importance of having good pictures, and some of the ways that you can attract some more followers to your page. In the end, you will be able to use Instagram to really bring in the customers without having to pay a lot of money to an Instagram expert.

When you want to expand your social media marketing campaign and you want to really get the high sales and engagement rates that come with Instagram, make sure to check out this guidebook and learn as much as you can about how to market your business on Instagram.